Type 2 Diabetes Cookbook
for Beginners

2000 Days of Super Easy, Delicious Low-Sugar & Low-Carb Recipes for Type 1 & Type 2 Diabetes, Prediabetes and Newly Diagnosed with a 30-Day Meal Plan | Full-Color Pictures

Savoring Healthy Living Without Compromising Taste

Julianna Wiggins

TABLE OF CONTENTS

INTRODUCTION

Dear Readers,

Welcome to the start of a transformative journey with "Type 2 Diabetes Cookbook for Beginners." Tailored for those with Type 2 Diabetes, Prediabetes, or for anyone looking to enjoy a healthier lifestyle, this cookbook is your key to balancing diabetes management with culinary enjoyment.

Within these pages lies not just a collection of recipes, but a new outlook on food, health, and diabetes management. We understand the daily concerns of living with diabetes – from monitoring blood sugar to finding joy in every meal. Our aim is to seamlessly integrate these challenges into a delicious, fulfilling life.

Our cookbook offers over 2000 days of easy, delightful low-sugar, low-carb recipes. Each dish is more than just ingredients and instructions; it's a step towards a healthier, more vibrant you. From energizing breakfasts to satisfying dinners and guilt-free desserts, these recipes cater to all tastes and dietary needs.

Your guide, Julianna Wiggins, combines her professional culinary expertise with a deep understanding of diabetic nutrition. Her recipes are not just tested for taste but also crafted to enhance your health and well-being. Julianna's philosophy is simple: managing diabetes shouldn't mean compromising on flavor or variety.

As you embark on this journey, imagine a life where managing diabetes is in harmony with enjoying delicious meals. Each page turned in this book is a step towards a healthier, more flavorful way of living.

Are you ready to embark on a more conscious and healthy lifestyle? Let's get started. Your journey to a healthier and tastier life begins right now.

Understanding Diabetes: An Overview of Diabetes and Its Impact on Nutrition

Welcome to Chapter 1, where we embark on a crucial journey to understand diabetes and its profound relationship with nutrition. Whether you or a loved one is navigating this condition, understanding diabetes is the first step toward effective management and a healthier lifestyle.

What is Diabetes?

Diabetes is a chronic condition characterized by high levels of sugar, or glucose, in the blood. It occurs when your body either doesn't produce enough insulin (a hormone that regulates blood sugar) or cannot effectively use the insulin it produces. This imbalance can lead to a range of health issues if not managed properly.

Types of Diabetes

Primarily, there are three types of diabetes:

Type 1 Diabetes: An autoimmune condition where the body attacks and destroys insulin-producing cells in the pancreas.
Type 2 Diabetes: The most common form, where the body either resists the effects of insulin or doesn't produce enough insulin to maintain a normal glucose level.
Gestational Diabetes: Occurs in pregnant women and typically resolves after childbirth, but it increases the risk of developing Type 2 diabetes later in life.

The Role of Nutrition in Diabetes Management

Nutrition plays a pivotal role in managing diabetes. The right diet can help control blood sugar levels, prevent complications, and maintain overall health. It's not just about cutting out sugar; it's about understanding which foods affect your blood sugar levels and how to balance them with insulin and other medications.

Carbohydrates and Blood Sugar

Carbohydrates have the most significant impact on blood sugar levels. Learning how to count carbohydrates and understand how different types of carbs affect your body is vital. This doesn't mean you have to give up all your favorite foods; it's about making informed choices and understanding portion sizes.

Healthy Fats and Proteins

Incorporating healthy fats and proteins into your diet is also crucial. They can help slow the absorption of carbohydrates, keeping blood sugar levels more stable.

Reading Food Labels

An essential skill you'll learn in this journey is reading and understanding food labels. It's not just about looking at the sugar content but also understanding other components like fiber, fats, and proteins that can influence your blood sugar levels.

The Big Picture

Managing diabetes is not just about adhering to a strict diet; it's about creating a balanced, enjoyable approach to eating that also respects your body's needs. This chapter sets the foundation for understanding how to live well with diabetes, and the rest of this book will build on this knowledge, offering delicious, diabetes-friendly recipes that align with these nutritional principles.

As we delve into the specifics of diabetes and nutrition, remember that knowledge is power. The more you understand about diabetes and how different foods affect your body, the better equipped you'll be to make choices that support your health and well-being.

Stay tuned as we take this journey together, transforming challenges into opportunities for healthful, joyous eating.

The Role of Diet in Diabetes Management: How Diet Can Help in Controlling Blood Sugar Levels

As we delve deeper into the intricacies of diabetes management, it becomes clear that diet plays a fundamental role. In fact, what you eat and when you eat can be as crucial as any medication. This section explores how a well-planned diet can be a powerful tool in controlling blood sugar levels and maintaining overall health.

Understanding the Glycemic Index

The Glycemic Index (GI) is a helpful guide for understanding how different foods affect blood sugar levels. Foods with a high GI raise blood sugar levels rapidly, while those with a low GI have a slower, more gradual effect. Integrating more low GI foods into your diet can help stabilize blood sugar levels.

Balancing Carbohydrates

Carbohydrates are often viewed as the enemy in diabetes management, but it's more about balance and type. Complex carbohydrates, like those found in whole grains, legumes, and vegetables, are absorbed more slowly and have less impact on blood sugar spikes. Learning to balance these with your insulin intake and physical activity is key.

The Importance of Fiber

High-fiber foods not only aid digestion but also help control blood sugar levels. Fiber slows the absorption of sugar into the bloodstream, preventing rapid spikes. Foods rich in fiber, such as fruits, vegetables, and whole grains, should be a staple in a diabetic diet.

Healthy Fats and Proteins

Incorporating healthy fats and proteins into your meals can also moderate blood sugar levels. Foods like fish, nuts, and seeds provide essential fatty acids and can help you feel full, reducing the likelihood of overeating.

Consistent Meal Timing

Regular meal times play a crucial role in diabetes management. Eating at regular intervals helps maintain steady blood sugar levels throughout the day. Skipping meals, especially breakfast, can lead to unpredictable blood sugar fluctuations.

Portion Control

Portion control is essential. Overeating, even healthy foods, can lead to weight gain and higher blood sugar levels. Using measuring tools or visual cues can help manage portion sizes effectively.

Here's a list of foods with a low glycemic index (GI) that can help stabilize blood sugar levels, ideal for an American audience:

Whole Grains: Opt for whole-grain breads, brown rice, quinoa, and whole oats. These grains have a lower GI compared to their refined counterparts.

Legumes: Beans, lentils, and chickpeas are excellent choices. They're not only low in GI but also high in fiber and protein.

Non-Starchy Vegetables: Include plenty of leafy greens like spinach and kale, as well as broccoli, cauliflower, and zucchini. These vegetables are low in carbohydrates and GI.

Nuts and Seeds: Almonds, walnuts, flaxseeds, and chia seeds are not only low GI but also a good source of healthy fats.

Whole Fruits: Though fruits contain sugar, many have a low GI. Apples, berries, oranges, and pears are good options. Remember to consume them whole rather than juiced to benefit from their fiber content.

Dairy and Dairy Alternatives: Plain yogurt, especially Greek yogurt, and low-fat milk or plant-based alternatives like almond milk can be part of a low-GI diet.

Pasta: Surprisingly, pasta, especially whole-grain or legume-based, can have a lower GI than other forms of wheat-based products due to its dense structure.

Remember, the key is portion control and balance. Incorporating these low-GI foods into your diet can help in managing blood sugar levels effectively.

Staying Hydrated

Proper hydration is critical. Water doesn't directly lower blood sugar levels, but it helps flush excess glucose through urine and prevents dehydration, which can affect blood sugar levels.

Personalized Diet Plans

Remember, there's no one-size-fits-all diet for diabetes. It's crucial to work with healthcare professionals to create a diet plan that's tailored to your individual needs, taking into account your lifestyle, medication, and any other health conditions.

In summary, a well-thought-out diet is a cornerstone of diabetes management. By understanding and implementing these dietary principles, you can take significant strides in controlling your blood sugar levels, reducing the risk of complications, and improving your overall quality of life. As we progress through this book, we'll explore how these principles come to life in delicious, healthful recipes.

Latest Research in Diabetes and Nutrition: A Review of Recent Scientific Discoveries

As we continue to explore the vital role of diet in managing diabetes, it is crucial to stay abreast of the latest research. Recent scientific discoveries have shed new light on how diet impacts diabetes, offering valuable insights for those seeking to control this condition through nutritional means.

The Impact of a Low-Carb Diet

Recent studies have highlighted the effectiveness of low-carb diets in managing Type 2 diabetes. By reducing carbohydrate intake, individuals can lower their blood sugar levels and improve their body's sensitivity to insulin. This approach has been shown to not only help in controlling blood glucose levels but also in reducing the need for medication in some cases. Foods that are part of a low-carb diet often include lean meats, fish, eggs, dairy products, non-starchy vegetables, and healthy fats.

The Importance of Whole Grains

Contrary to the approach of a strictly low-carb diet, numerous studies have emphasized the benefits of including whole grains in a diabetic diet. Whole grains, unlike their refined counterparts, are rich in fiber and have a lower glycemic index. This means they have a less dramatic effect on blood sugar levels. Regular consumption of whole grains like brown rice, barley, and whole wheat has been associated with a reduced risk of developing Type 2 diabetes and better blood sugar control.

Balancing Macro- and Micronutrients

Balancing macronutrients (carbohydrates, proteins, and fats) and micronutrients (vitamins and minerals) is essential in diabetes management. Cutting-edge research underscores the significance of this balance. A diet that includes a variety of foods can ensure

an adequate intake of essential nutrients. For example, magnesium, found in leafy greens and nuts, has been linked to improved insulin sensitivity, while sufficient dietary fiber intake is known to support blood sugar control and gastrointestinal health.

Personalized Nutrition Plans

An emerging area of research is the field of personalized nutrition. It's becoming increasingly clear that dietary plans for diabetes management should be tailored to the individual. Factors like age, lifestyle, and the presence of other health conditions play a role in determining the most effective dietary approach. Personalized nutrition plans consider these variables, offering more targeted and effective dietary recommendations.

In conclusion, staying informed about the latest research in diabetes and nutrition empowers individuals to make educated dietary choices. Whether it's adopting a low-carb diet, incorporating whole grains, or balancing nutrients, the key is finding a sustainable and enjoyable eating plan that supports diabetes management.

Understanding Carbohydrates: Carbohydrates and Their Impact on Blood Sugar Levels

In the realm of diabetes management, understanding carbohydrates is pivotal. Carbohydrates, commonly referred to as carbs, play a significant role in influencing blood sugar levels, making their management key for anyone with diabetes.

What are Carbohydrates?

Carbohydrates are one of the three primary macronutrients found in foods and drinks, alongside protein and fat. They are the body's main source of energy. Carbs are found in a wide range of foods, including fruits, vegetables, breads, pastas, and dairy products, as well as in sugary foods and drinks.

Types of Carbohydrates

Carbohydrates are classified into two main types: simple and complex. Simple carbohydrates, or sugars, are found naturally in foods such as fruit (fructose) and milk (lactose) or added to foods such as sodas, candies, and baked goods. Complex carbohydrates include whole grain breads, cereals, starchy vegetables, and legumes. They are composed of longer chains of sugar molecules, which generally means they take longer to digest and have a more gradual effect on blood sugar.

Carbohydrates and Blood Sugar

When you eat foods containing carbohydrates, your body breaks down the sugars and starches into glucose, which then enters your bloodstream. This increase in blood glucose signals the pancreas to produce insulin, a hormone that helps glucose enter the body's cells for energy. For people with diabetes, this process doesn't work as efficiently, leading to elevated blood sugar levels.

Glycemic Index and Glycemic Load

The glycemic index (GI) and glycemic load (GL) are tools that can help understand how different carbohydrate-containing foods affect blood sugar levels. GI measures how quickly a carbohydrate-containing food raises blood sugar, while GL takes into account the GI as well as the amount of carbohydrates in a serving of the food. Foods with a low GI or GL have a less immediate impact on blood sugar levels.

Balancing Carbohydrates in Your Diet

Managing carbohydrate intake is crucial for blood sugar control. This doesn't mean you need to avoid carbohydrates altogether. Instead, it's about choosing the right types of carbohydrates and balancing them with protein and healthy fats. Incorporating complex carbohydrates with a lower GI can help maintain steady blood sugar levels. Additionally, portion control and consistent meal timing play an essential role in managing the impact of carbohydrates on blood sugar.

In summary, understanding and managing carbohydrate intake is a cornerstone of diabetes management. By choosing the right types and amounts of carbohydrates and pairing them with other macronutrients, you can enjoy a varied diet while keeping your blood sugar levels in check. The following chapters will provide you with practical tips and delicious recipes that incorporate these principles, helping you manage your diabetes deliciously and healthfully.

Choosing Healthy Fats and Proteins: How to Integrate Beneficial Fats and Proteins into Your Diet

In managing diabetes, it's not only the carbohydrates in your diet that matter. Fats and proteins play a crucial role too. Understanding how to integrate healthy fats and quality proteins into your diet can significantly enhance blood sugar control and overall health.

The Role of Fats in Your Diet

Fats have long been misunderstood, but they are an essential part of a healthy diet, especially for individuals with diabetes. They are a source of energy and help in the absorption of certain vitamins. However, the type of fat you choose is key.

Healthy Fats: These include monounsaturated and polyunsaturated fats, found in foods like olive oil, avocados, nuts, seeds, and fatty fish like salmon and mackerel. These fats can help improve blood cholesterol levels and reduce the risk of heart disease, which is particularly important for people with diabetes.

Limit Saturated and Trans Fats: Saturated fats, found in red meat, butter, and dairy products, and trans fats, often found in processed foods, should be consumed in moderation. These types of fats can raise cholesterol levels and increase the risk of heart disease.

The Importance of Protein

Proteins are vital for repairing and building tissues, and they play a crucial role in how the body processes carbohydrates.

Quality Protein Sources: Include lean meats, poultry, fish, eggs, dairy products, beans, legumes, and nuts in your diet. These sources provide essential amino acids without the added saturated fats.

Protein and Blood Sugar Control: Proteins have a minimal impact on blood sugar levels. They can also help you feel fuller for longer, which can aid in weight management – an important aspect of diabetes control.

Balancing Fats and Proteins with Carbohydrates

Incorporating a balance of healthy fats and proteins with carbohydrates can help slow the absorption of sugar into your bloodstream, leading to more stable blood sugar levels.

Meal Planning: Try to include a source of protein and healthy fat at each meal. For example, add nuts to your morning oatmeal, enjoy a salad with olive oil dressing and grilled chicken for lunch, and have baked salmon with a side of roasted vegetables for dinner.

Snacking Smart: Choose snacks that include a balance of carbs, protein, and fat. A great example would be apple slices with almond butter or a small serving of cheese with whole-grain crackers.

In conclusion, incorporating healthy fats and quality proteins into your diet is not just about managing diabetes; it's about enhancing overall health and well-being. By making informed choices about the fats and proteins you consume, you can enjoy a diverse, satisfying, and diabetes-friendly diet. The upcoming chapters will provide you with delicious recipes that perfectly balance these macronutrients, helping you to manage your diabetes with every meal.

Reading and Understanding Food Labels: Learn How to Choose the Right Products

Navigating the world of food labels can be a daunting task, especially for those managing diabetes. Understanding how to read and interpret these labels is crucial for making informed dietary choices.

Ingredients to Avoid

When reading food labels, it's just as important to know which ingredients to avoid as it is to understand what to look for. Here are some key ingredients those with diabetes should be wary of:

High Fructose Corn Syrup and Other Sweeteners: High fructose corn syrup, agave nectar, cane sugar, and other sweeteners can quickly raise blood sugar levels. Even 'natural' sweeteners can have this effect.

Trans Fats: Often labeled as "partially hydrogenated oils," trans fats are harmful to heart health, a major concern for those with diabetes.

Excessive Sodium: High sodium levels can lead to hypertension, a common issue in diabetics. Processed and canned foods often have high sodium content, so it's better to opt for fresh or frozen alternatives.

Artificial Additives: These include artificial colors, flavors, and preservatives, such as aspartame, MSG (monosodium glutamate), and sulfites. While they may not directly impact blood sugar levels, they can have other adverse health effects.

Refined Grains: Ingredients like white flour or white rice indicate the product is made with refined grains, which can have similar blood sugar effects as sugar.

Saturated Fats: While not as harmful as trans fats, saturated fats should still be consumed in moderation. They're commonly found in animal products and some plant oils.

By avoiding these ingredients, you can make healthier choices that align with diabetes management goals and overall well-being. Remember, the best foods for diabetes management are those closest to their natural state – fresh fruits and vegetables, whole grains, lean proteins, and healthy fats.

Deciphering the Nutrition Facts Label

Every packaged food comes with a Nutrition Facts label, which provides vital information about the product's nutritional content.

Serving Size and Servings Per Container: This is your starting point. All the nutritional information on the label is based on this serving size. Be mindful of how many servings you are actually consuming.

Total Carbohydrates: Pay close attention to this section, as it directly impacts blood sugar levels. It includes dietary fiber, sugars, and added sugars. Remember, it's not just about the amount of carbohydrates but also the type.

Dietary Fiber: High-fiber foods can help control blood sugar levels. The fiber content is included under total carbohydrates, and higher fiber content is generally better.

Sugars and Added Sugars: Naturally occurring sugars and added sugars are also listed here. Minimizing added sugars is essential for diabetes management.

Protein: Check the protein content, especially if you are balancing carbohydrate intake with proteins to manage blood sugar levels.

Fat: Look at the type and amount of fat present. Focus on foods with healthy fats like monounsaturated and polyunsaturated fats.

Ingredients List

The ingredients list is equally important. Ingredients are listed in descending order by weight. This means that the first few ingredients are the most predominant.

Look for Whole Foods: Choose products with whole foods like whole grains, lean meats, or whole fruits as the first ingredients.

Avoid Unhealthy Additives: Be wary of products with long lists of unrecognizable ingredients, which often include unhealthy additives and preservatives.

Understand Sugar Content: Various terms are used for added sugars (like corn syrup, sucrose, dextrose, etc.). Recognizing these terms can help you make healthier choices.

Health Claims and Labels

Be cautious of health claims on packaging. Phrases like "low-fat" or "sugar-free" can be misleading. A product labeled as "sugar-free" might still contain carbohydrates or unhealthy artificial sweeteners.

Putting It into Practice

Start practicing your label-reading skills during your next grocery shopping trip. With time, you'll become more adept at quickly identifying the healthiest options for your dietary needs.

In essence, understanding food labels is a key skill in diabetes management and overall healthful eating. As you progress through this book, you'll find that choosing the right products becomes second nature, making your journey with diabetes more manageable and enjoyable.

CHAPTER 2: 30-DAY MEAL PLAN

Day	Breakfast	Lunch	Snack	Dinner
Day 1	Buckwheat Porridge (380 kcal) - p.18	Greek Avgolemono Soup (350 kcal) - p.32	Vegan Banana Toffee (150 kcal) - p.45	Red Fish Tartlets with Cottage Cheese (400 kcal) - p.58
Day 2	Cottage Cheese Bowl (380 kcal) - p.18	Creamy Chicken and Mushroom Soup (350 kcal) - p.32	Stevia-Sweetened Lemon Tart (150 kcal) - p.45	Mediterranean Tuna and White Bean Salad (400 kcal) - p.58
Day 3	Cauliflower Rice Breakfast Bowl (350 kcal) - p.19	Hungarian Goulash Soup (350 kcal) - p.33	Avocado and Blueberry Trifle (160 kcal) - p.46	Grilled Salmon with Avocado Salsa (450 kcal) - p.59
Day 4	Baked Cheese Pancakes with Coconut Flour and Berries (350 kcal) - p.19	Chicken Dumpling Soup (330 kcal) - p.33	Low-Calorie Chocolate Mousse with Chicory and Raspberry (180 kcal) - p.46	Grilled Tuna Steaks with Olive Tapenade (450 kcal) - p.59
Day 5	Zucchini and Corn Pancakes (350 kcal) - p.20	Beef Medallions with Mustard Sauce (460 kcal) - p.34	Chia Pudding with Avocado (200 kcal) - p.47	Fish Stew with Shrimp and Coconut Milk (420 kcal) - p.60
Day 6	Egg Muffins with Veggies (400 kcal) - p.20	Beef Rolls with Cheese and Asparagus (450 kcal) - p.34	Coconut Flour Brownies (160 kcal) - p.47	Classic Marinated Fish Recipe (350 kcal) - p.60
Day 7	Protein-Packed Breakfast Burrito (330 kcal) - p.21	Pork with Mushrooms and Bell Peppers in Cream Sauce (460 kcal) - p.35	Sugar-Free Apple Mousse (140 kcal) - p.48	Lemon-Garlic Shrimp with Zucchini Noodles (410 kcal) - p.61
Day 8	Baked Oatmeal Cups (350 kcal) - p.21	Herb-Crusted Pork with Roasted Zucchini (450 kcal) - p.35	Keto Dark Chocolate Truffles (160 kcal) - p.48	Chopped Red Fish Patties (420 kcal) - p.61
Day 9	Apple and Walnut Baked Oatmeal (350 kcal) - p.22	Warm Pork and Vegetable Salad (430 kcal) - p.36	Chocolate Chip Cookies (170 kcal) - p.49	Couscous with Fish and Tomatoes (320 kcal) - p.62

Day	Breakfast	Lunch	Snack	Dinner
Day 10	Spinach and Feta Omelet (400 kcal) - p.22	Mushroom Soup with Cheese (300 kcal) - p.36	Healthy Chocolate Banana Candies (100 kcal) - p.49	White Fish in Creamy Garlic Sauce (370 kcal) - p.62
Day 11	Muffins with Zucchini and Cheese (400 kcal) - p.23	Braised Beef with Vegetables and Thyme (450 kcal) - p.37	Cinnamon Spiced Baked Pears (150 kcal) - p.50	Salad with Marinated Mussels (250 kcal) - p.63
Day 12	Quinoa with Almonds and Berries (350 kcal) - p.23	Beef and Vegetable Minestrone (440 kcal) - p.37	Healthy Peanut Butter Baskets (160 kcal) - p.50	Butterfish Steak with Vegetables (420 kcal) - p.63
Day 13	Lavash Roll with Cottage Cheese and Herbs (380 kcal) - p.24	Chicken Piccata with Capers (420 kcal) - p.38	No-Sugar-Added Berry Sorbet (140 kcal) - p.51	Squid Salad with Mushrooms and Mozzarella (230 kcal) - p.64
Day 14	Ricotta and Tomato Toast (350 kcal) - p.24	Herbed Turkey and Quinoa Stuffed Bell Peppers (440 kcal) - p.38	Sugar-Free Blueberry Almond Clafoutis (160 kcal) - p.51	Cajun Shrimp and Cauliflower Grits (420 kcal) - p.64
Day 15	Chicken, Spinach, and Tomato Frittata (380 kcal) - p.25	Lamb Meatballs with Tzatziki Sauce (450 kcal) - p.39	Ricotta and Berry Stuffed Crepes (170 kcal) - p.52	Arugula Salad with Cherry Tomatoes and Mussels (350 kcal) - p.65
Day 16	Protein-Packed Breakfast Burrito (400 kcal) - p.21	Spiced Duck Breast with Orange Glaze (460 kcal) - p.39	Keto-Friendly Tiramisu (180 kcal) - p.52	Zucchini Rolls with Fish and Shrimp (320 kcal) - p.65
Day 17	Banana Peanut Butter Smoothie (350 kcal) - p.25	Spiced Lamb Skewers with Greek Yogurt Dip (470 kcal) - p.40	Low-Carb Pumpkin Cheesecake (150 kcal) - p.53	Fried Mussels (220 kcal) - p.66
Day 18	Greek Yogurt Parfait (350 kcal) - p.26	Buckwheat Patties with Cheese and Mushrooms (430 kcal) - p.40	Baked Ricotta with Lemon and Thyme (140 kcal) - p.53	Rice with Squid and Egg (350 kcal) - p.66
Day 19	Tacos with Scrambled Eggs (380 kcal) - p.26	Baked Chicken Breast with Tomatoes and Mozzarella (450 kcal) - p.41	Nutritious Date Candies (150 kcal) - p.54	Creamy Fish and Broccoli Quiche Baked in the Oven (450 kcal) - p.67

Day	Breakfast	Lunch	Snack	Dinner
Day 20	Quinoa Breakfast Bowl (380 kcal) - p.27	Chicken Legs in Keto Honey Sauce (420 kcal) - p.41	Egg-Free Berry Cheesecake (100 kcal) - p.54	Fish in Parchment with Cherry Tomatoes (300 kcal) - p.68
Day 21	Berry and Nut Smoothie (350 kcal) - p.27	Chicken Drumsticks with Spicy Chimichurri Sauce (440 kcal) - p.42	Low-Carb Lemon Cheesecake Bars (160 kcal) - p.55	Blue Pancakes Stuffed with Fish Filling (450 kcal) - p.68
Day 22	Mushroom and Spinach Frittata (350 kcal) - p.28	Chicken Soup with Cauliflower and Thyme (300 kcal) - p.42	Light Coffee Cheesecake without Sugar (150 kcal) - p.55	Creamy Mussel Soup (380 kcal) - p.69
Day 23	Cheese and Egg Waffles (380 kcal) - p.28	Chicken, Avocado, and Walnut Salad (410 kcal) - p.43	Oat Baskets with Cottage Cheese and Berries (120 kcal) - p.56	Glass Noodle Seafood Stir-Fry (320 kcal) - p.69
Day 24	Veggie Breakfast Scramble (350 kcal) - p.29	Asian Beef Salad with Sesame Dressing (440 kcal) - p.43	Cottage Cheese Dessert with Blueberries (160 kcal) - p.56	Classic Seafood Paella (450 kcal) - p.70
Day 25	Low-Carb Blueberry Muffins (350 kcal) - p.29	Buckwheat-Stuffed Chicken (510 kcal) - p.44	Baked Apples with Cottage Cheese (140 kcal) - p.57	Fish in Parchment with Cherry Tomatoes (300 kcal) - p.68
Day 26	Chia Seed Pudding (350 kcal) - p.30	Warm Pork and Vegetable Salad (440 kcal) - p.36	Sugar-Free Apple Mousse (140 kcal) - p.48	Grilled Tuna Steaks with Olive Tapenade (450 kcal) - p.59
Day 27	Homemade Caramel Granola with Coconut Flour and Berries (380 kcal) - p.30	Mushroom Soup with Cheese (300 kcal) - p.36	Low-Carb Lemon Cheesecake Bars (160 kcal) - p.55	Cajun Shrimp and Cauliflower Grits (420 kcal) - p.64
Day 28	Kale and White Bean Hash (350 kcal) - p.31	Pork with Mushrooms and Bell Peppers in Cream Sauce (450 kcal) - p.35	No-Sugar-Added Berry Sorbet (140 kcal) - p.51	Arugula Salad with Cherry Tomatoes and Mussels (350 kcal) - p.65

Day	Breakfast	Lunch	Snack	Dinner
Day 29	Oatmeal with Flaxseeds (350 kcal) - p.31	Braised Beef with Vegetables and Thyme (460 kcal) - p.37	Keto Dark Chocolate Truffles (160 kcal) - p.48	Salad with Marinated Mussels (250 kcal) - p.63
Day 30	Spinach and Feta Omelet (330 kcal) - p.22	Herb-Crusted Pork with Roasted Zucchini (430 kcal) - p.35	Cinnamon Spiced Baked Pears (150 kcal) - p.50	Creamy Mussel Soup (380 kcal) - p.69

Note: We wish to remind you that the 30-Day Meal Plan provided in this book is intended as a guide and a source of inspiration. The caloric content of the dishes is approximate and may vary depending on the portion sizes and specific ingredients. This plan represents a diverse, balanced menu, combining a richness of proteins, healthy fats, and minimal carbohydrates. It allows for following a low-carb diet while enjoying delicious and nutritious meals every day.

If you find that the calories in the recipes do not completely align with your personal needs or the plan, feel free to adjust the portion sizes. Increase or decrease them to ensure that the meal plan suits your individual goals and preferences. Be creative and enjoy each dish according to your needs!

CHAPTER 3: BREAKFASTS: Low-carb and balanced options to start your day

Buckwheat Porridge

Prep time: 5 minutes | Cook Time: 15 minutes | Serves: 1

Ingredients:

- ½ cup buckwheat groats (90g)
- 1 cup unsweetened almond milk (240ml)
- 1 small banana, sliced (90g)
- Pinch of cinnamon (optional)
- 1 tbsp chopped nuts (walnuts or almonds) for topping (15g)

Instructions:

1. In a small saucepan, bring the almond milk to a boil.
2. Add the buckwheat groats and reduce the heat to low. Simmer, covered, for 12-15 minutes or until the buckwheat is tender and the liquid is mostly absorbed.
3. Stir in cinnamon if using.
4. Topped with sliced banana and chopped nuts.

Nutritional Information (Per Serving): Calories: 290 | Fat: 14g | Protein: 14g | Carbohydrates: 28g | Sugars: 2g | Fiber: 12g | Sodium: 320mg.

Cottage Cheese Bowl

Prep Time: 5 minutes | Cook Time: 0 minutes | Serves: 1

Ingredients:

- 1 cup low-fat cottage cheese (225g)
- ½ cup cucumber, diced (approximately 75g)
- ½ cup cherry tomatoes, halved (approximately 75g)
- A pinch of black pepper
- Fresh herbs like dill or parsley, chopped (optional)

Instructions:

1. In a bowl, combine the cottage cheese with diced cucumber and halved cherry tomatoes.
2. Season with black pepper and optionally, fresh herbs.

Nutritional Information (Per Serving): Calories: 225 | Fat: 3.5g | Protein: 28g | Carbohydrates: 14g | Sugars: 8g | Fiber: 2g | Sodium: 650mg.

Cauliflower Rice Breakfast Bowl

Prep Time: 10 minutes | Cook Time: 15 minutes | Serves: 2

Ingredients:

- 2 cups cauliflower rice (fresh or frozen) (200g)
- ½ cup bell peppers, diced (75g)
- ¼ cup onions, diced (40g)
- 2 large eggs
- 1 tbsp olive oil (15ml)
- Salt and pepper to taste
- Optional toppings: avocado slices, salsa, low-fat cheese

Instructions:

1. Heat olive oil in a large skillet over medium heat.
2. Add onions and bell peppers, sautéing until soft.
3. Add cauliflower rice to the skillet, season with salt and pepper, and cook for about 5–7 minutes, or until tender.
4. Make two wells in the cauliflower rice and crack an egg into each. Cover and cook until the eggs are set to your liking.
5. Serve hot, with optional toppings like avocado, salsa, or cheese.

Nutritional Information (Per Serving): Calories: 260 | Fat: 16g | Protein: 10g | Carbohydrates: 18g | Sugars: 7g | Fiber: 5g | Sodium: 350mg.

Baked Cheese Pancakes with Coconut Flour and Berries

Prep time: 15 minutes | Cook Time: 20 minutes | Serves: 4

Ingredients:

- 1 ½ cups low-fat cottage cheese (340g)
- 2 large eggs
- ½ cup coconut flour (60g)
- 2 tbsp low-carb sweetener (30g)
- 1 tsp vanilla extract (5ml)
- ½ tsp baking powder
- ½ cup mixed berries (blueberries, raspberries, strawberries) (70g)
- Non-stick cooking spray

Instructions:

1. Preheat your oven to 350°F (175°C). Line a baking sheet with parchment paper and lightly spray with non-stick cooking spray.
2. In a large bowl, combine cottage cheese, eggs, coconut flour, low-carb sweetener, vanilla extract, and baking powder. Mix until well combined.
3. Gently fold in the mixed berries.
4. Form the mixture into small patties and place them on the prepared baking sheet.
5. Bake in the preheated oven for 18–20 minutes or until golden and firm.
6. Serve warm, optionally with a dollop of Greek yogurt or additional fresh berries.

Nutritional Information (Per Serving): Calories: 190 | Fat: 7g | Protein: 17g | Carbohydrates: 14g | Sugars: 3g | Fiber: 7g | Sodium: 400mg

Zucchini and Corn Pancakes

Prep time: 15 minutes | Cook Time: 20 minutes | Serves: 2

Ingredients:

- 1 cup zucchini, grated and excess moisture squeezed out (120g)
- ½ cup corn kernels (fresh or frozen and thawed) (75g)
- ¼ cup whole wheat flour (30g)
- 1 large egg
- 2 tbsp low-fat milk (30ml)
- ½ tsp baking powder
- Salt and pepper, to taste
- Olive oil for cooking

Instructions:

1. In a bowl, mix together the grated zucchini, corn, flour, egg, milk, baking powder, salt, and pepper until well combined.
2. Heat a non-stick skillet with a bit of olive oil over medium heat.
3. Pour spoonfuls of the batter into the skillet, flattening with the back of the spoon to form pancakes.
4. Cook until golden brown on each side, about 3-4 minutes per side.
5. Serve hot as a delicious and healthy meal option.

Nutritional Information (Per Serving): Calories: 220 | Fat: 6g | Protein: 8g | Carbohydrates: 35g | Sugars: 3g | Fiber: 5g | Sodium: 350mg.

Egg Muffins with Veggies

Prep Time: 10 minutes | Cook Time: 20 minutes | Serves: 6 (1 muffin per serving)

Ingredients:

- 6 large eggs
- ½ cup spinach, chopped (15g)
- ¼ cup mushrooms, diced (approximately 35g)
- ¼ cup bell peppers, diced (approximately 37g)
- ¼ cup low-fat cheese, shredded (28g)
- Salt and pepper, to taste
- Non-stick cooking spray

Instructions:

1. Preheat the oven to 350°F (175°C). Spray a muffin tin with non-stick cooking spray.
2. In a bowl, whisk the eggs. Stir in the spinach, mushrooms, bell peppers, and cheese. Season with salt and pepper.
3. Pour the mixture into the muffin tin, filling each cup about two-thirds full.
4. Bake for 18-20 minutes or until the egg muffins are set and lightly golden on top.
5. Let cool for a few minutes before removing from the tin. Serve warm.

Nutritional Information (Per Serving): Calories: 220 (for 2 muffins) | Fat: 6g | Protein: 7g | Carbohydrates: 2g | Sugars: 1g | Fiber: 0.5g | Sodium: 160mg

Protein-Packed Breakfast Burrito

Prep Time: 10 minutes | Cook Time: 10 minutes | Serves: 1

Ingredients:

- 1 whole wheat tortilla
- 2 egg whites
- ¼ cup black beans, drained and rinsed (approximately 45g)
- 2 tbsp salsa (30g)
- ¼ cup shredded low-fat cheese (28g)
- ¼ cup bell peppers, diced (approximately 37g)
- Non-stick cooking spray
- Salt and pepper, to taste

Instructions:

1. Spray a skillet with non-stick cooking spray and heat over medium heat.
2. Scramble the egg whites with salt and pepper, then add the bell peppers and black beans. Cook until the eggs are set.
3. Warm the tortilla in the microwave or on a skillet.
4. Place the egg mixture in the center of the tortilla, top with salsa and cheese.
5. Fold the sides of the tortilla in, then roll up to form a burrito.
6. Serve warm.

Nutritional Information (Per Serving): Calories: 320 | Fat: 8g | Protein: 24g | Carbohydrates: 40g | Sugars: 3g | Fiber: 9g | Sodium: 650mg.

Baked Oatmeal Cups

Prep Time: 15 minutes | Cook Time: 20 minutes | Serves: 6 (1 cup per serving)

Ingredients:

- 2 cups rolled oats (160g)
- 1 tsp baking powder
- ½ tsp cinnamon
- Pinch of salt
- 1 cup unsweetened almond milk (240ml)
- 1 large egg
- ¼ cup honey or maple syrup (60ml)
- ½ cup mixed nuts, chopped (walnuts, almonds) (60g)
- ½ cup dried fruit (raisins, cranberries) (80g)

Instructions:

1. Preheat oven to 350°F (175°C). Line a muffin tin with paper liners or grease with non-stick spray.
2. In a large bowl, mix together oats, baking powder, cinnamon, and salt.
3. In another bowl, whisk together almond milk, egg, and honey or maple syrup.
4. Combine the wet ingredients with the dry ingredients, then fold in the nuts and dried fruit.
5. Divide the mixture into the muffin tin and bake for 20 minutes or until the tops are golden brown.
6. Let cool before serving. These are perfect for a grab-and-go breakfast.

Nutritional Information (Per Serving): Calories: 260 | Fat: 10g | Protein: 6g | Carbohydrates: 39g | Sugars: 17g | Fiber: 4g | Sodium: 190mg.

Apple and Walnut Baked Oatmeal

Prep Time: 10 minutes | Cook Time: 25 minutes | Serves: 4

Ingredients:

- 2 cups rolled oats (160g)
- 1 tsp baking powder
- ½ tsp cinnamon
- Pinch of salt
- 1 cup unsweetened almond milk (240ml)
- 2 tbsp sugar-free syrup (30ml)
- 1 large egg
- 1 large apple, diced (180g)
- ½ cup walnuts, chopped (50g)

Instructions:

1. Preheat oven to 375°F (190°C). Grease an 8-inch square baking dish.
2. In a bowl, mix together oats, baking powder, cinnamon, and salt.
3. In another bowl, whisk together almond milk, sugar-free syrup or sugar substitute, and egg.
4. Stir the wet ingredients into the dry ingredients, then fold in the diced apple and walnuts.
5. Pour the mixture into the prepared dish and bake for 25 minutes or until golden brown and set.
6. Serve warm, optionally with a dollop of Greek yogurt.

Nutritional Information (Per Serving): Calories: 330 | Fat: 14g | Protein: 8g | Carbohydrates: 35g | Sugars: 7g | Fiber: 7g | Sodium: 220mg.

Spinach and Feta Omelet

Prep Time: 5 minutes | Cook Time: 10 minutes | Serves: 1

Ingredients:

- 2 large eggs
- ½ cup fresh spinach, chopped (15g)
- ¼ cup feta cheese, crumbled (50g)
- 1 tbsp olive oil (15ml)
- Salt and pepper, to taste

Instructions:

1. Beat the eggs in a bowl, season with salt and pepper.
2. Heat olive oil in a non-stick skillet over medium heat.
3. Pour the eggs into the skillet. Once they begin to set, add spinach and feta cheese on one half of the omelet.
4. Gently fold the other half over the filling. Cook until the eggs are set and the cheese begins to melt, about 2-3 minutes.
5. Carefully slide the omelet onto a plate and serve hot.

Nutritional Information (Per Serving): Calories: 350 | Fat: 28g | Protein: 20g | Carbohydrates: 4g | Sugars: 1g | Fiber: 1g | Sodium: 600mg.

Muffins with Zucchini and Cheese

Quinoa with Almonds and Berries

Prep Time: 15 minutes | Cook Time: 20 minutes | Serves: 6 (1 muffin per serving)

Prep Time: 5 minutes | Cook Time: 20 minutes | Serves: 2

Ingredients:

- 1 cup whole wheat flour (120g)
- 1 tsp baking powder
- ½ tsp salt
- 2 large eggs
- ¼ cup olive oil (60ml)
- ½ cup low-fat milk (120ml)
- 1 cup zucchini, grated and excess moisture squeezed out (120g)
- ½ cup low-fat cheddar cheese, shredded (56g)

Ingredients:

- ½ cup quinoa, rinsed (85g)
- 1 cup unsweetened almond milk (240ml)
- 1 tbsp sugar-free syrup (15ml)
- ½ cup mixed berries (blueberries, strawberries, raspberries) (70g)
- ¼ cup almonds, sliced or chopped (30g)

Instructions:

1. Preheat oven to 350°F (175°C). Line a muffin tin with paper liners or grease with non-stick spray.
2. In a large bowl, combine flour, baking powder, and salt.
3. In another bowl, whisk together eggs, olive oil, and milk. Add this to the dry ingredients and stir until just combined.
4. Fold in grated zucchini and cheddar cheese.
5. Divide the batter evenly among the muffin cups.
6. Bake for 20 minutes or until a toothpick inserted into the center comes out clean.
7. Cool in the pan for 5 minutes, then transfer to a wire rack.

Instructions:

1. In a small saucepan, combine quinoa and almond milk. Bring to a boil, then reduce heat to low and simmer, covered, for 15 minutes or until quinoa is cooked and liquid is absorbed.
2. Stir in the sugar-free syrup or sugar substitute to taste.
3. Serve in bowls, topped with mixed berries and almonds.

Nutritional Information (Per Serving): Calories: 320 | Fat: 10g | Protein: 9g | Carbohydrates: 35g | Sugars: 10g | Fiber: 7g | Sodium: 160mg

Nutritional Information (Per Serving): Calories: 260 | Fat: 14g | Protein: 8g | Carbohydrates: 25g | Sugars: 2g | Fiber: 3g | Sodium: 380mg.

Lavash Roll with Cottage Cheese and Herbs

Prep Time: 15 minutes | Cook Time: 15 minutes | Serves: 2

Ingredients:

- 1 large sheet of lavash bread (about 2/3 of a standard sheet)
- 2/3 cup low-fat cottage cheese (0% fat) (150g)
- 2 tbsp fresh parsley, chopped
- Salt and spices to taste (e.g., garlic powder, paprika, black pepper)
- 1 egg yolk, lightly beaten
- Optional: sesame seeds, flaxseeds, or poppy seeds for topping

Instructions:

1. Preheat your oven to 375°F (190°C). Line a baking sheet with parchment paper.
2. Add the chopped parsley, salt, and your choice of spices to the cottage cheese. Mix well and adjust seasoning as needed.
3. Spread the lavash bread on a flat surface. Evenly distribute the cottage cheese mixture over the lavash.
4. Carefully roll up the lavash, tucking in the edges to prevent the filling from leaking. Place the roll on the prepared baking sheet.
5. Brush the top with the beaten egg yolk and sprinkle with your choice of seeds if desired.
6. Bake in the preheated oven for 12-15 minutes, or until the lavash is golden and crispy.

Nutritional Information (Per Serving): Calories: 285 | Fat: 7g | Protein: 19g | Carbohydrates: 36g | Sugars: 2g | Fiber: 3g | Sodium: 580mg.

Ricotta and Tomato Toast

Prep Time: 5 minutes | Cook Time: 0 minutes | Serves: 1

Ingredients:

- 1 slice whole grain bread
- 1/3 cup ricotta cheese (82g)
- 1 small tomato, sliced (90g)
- A sprinkle of fresh basil, chopped
- Salt and pepper, to taste
- Drizzle of olive oil (optional)

Instructions:

1. Toast the bread slice to your desired level of crispiness.
2. Spread the ricotta cheese evenly over the toast.
3. Arrange tomato slices on top of the ricotta.
4. Season with salt, pepper, and a sprinkle of fresh basil.
5. Optionally, drizzle a bit of olive oil over the top.
6. Serve immediately for a healthy and refreshing breakfast or snack.

Nutritional Information (Per Serving): Calories: 280 | Fat: 15g | Protein: 13g | Carbohydrates: 25g | Sugars: 4g | Fiber: 4g | Sodium: 360mg.

Chicken, Spinach, and Tomato Frittata

Prep Time: 15 minutes | Cook Time: 20 minutes | Serves: 4

Ingredients:

- 4 large eggs
- 10.5 oz chicken breast, cooked and diced (300g)
- 7 oz tomatoes, diced (200g)
- 6 oz bell pepper, diced (170g)
- 3.5 oz onion, diced (100g)
- ¼ cup coconut milk (60ml)
- 1.75 oz fresh spinach (50g)
- 1 oz Parmesan cheese, grated (28g)
- 2 tbsp vegetable oil (30ml)
- 1 tsp dried tomato pieces
- 1 tsp Italian seasoning
- Salt and black pepper, to taste

Instructions:

1. Preheat the oven to 375°F (190°C).
2. In a large mixing bowl, whisk together the eggs, coconut milk, Italian seasoning, dried tomato pieces, salt, and pepper.
3. Heat the vegetable oil in an oven-safe skillet over medium heat. Sauté the onions and bell peppers until soft.
4. Add the diced chicken and cook for a few more minutes. Add the spinach and cook until it wilts.
5. Pour the egg mixture over the cooked ingredients in the skillet. Sprinkle with Parmesan cheese.
6. Cook on the stove for about 3-4 minutes until the edges begin to set.
7. Transfer the skillet to the oven and bake for 12-15 minutes or until the frittata is set and lightly golden.
8. Let it cool slightly before slicing and serving.

Nutritional Information (Per Serving): Calories: 295 | Fat: 16g | Protein: 27g | Carbohydrates: 9g | Sugars: 3g | Fiber: 2g | Sodium: 390mg.

Banana Peanut Butter Smoothie

Prep Time: 5 minutes | Cook Time: 0 minutes | Serves: 1

Ingredients:

- 1 medium ripe banana
- 1 tbsp natural peanut butter (16g)
- 1 cup unsweetened almond milk (240ml)
- ½ scoop unflavored or low-carb protein powder (optional) (15g)
- Ice cubes (optional)

Instructions:

1. Place the banana, peanut butter, unsweetened almond milk, and unflavored or low-carb protein powder (if using) in a blender.
2. Blend on high until smooth. Add ice cubes for a thicker, colder smoothie if desired.
3. Pour into a glass and enjoy as a nutritious and filling breakfast or snack.

Nutritional Information (Per Serving): Calories: 225 | Fat: 9g | Protein: 8g | Carbohydrates: 25g | Sugars: 10g | Fiber: 5g | Sodium: 240mg.

Greek Yogurt Parfait

Prep Time: 5 minutes | Cook Time: 0 minutes | Serves: 1

Ingredients:

- 1 cup plain Greek yogurt (245g)
- ½ cup mixed berries (blueberries, strawberries, raspberries) (70g)
- ¼ cup high-fiber granola (about 30g)
- Stevia or another sugar substitute to taste (optional)

Instructions:

1. In a bowl or glass, layer half of the Greek yogurt.
2. Add a layer of mixed berries, then sprinkle with half of the granola.
3. Repeat the layers with the remaining yogurt, berries, and granola.
4. If you desire additional sweetness, you can add a sugar substitute like stevia to taste.
5. Serve immediately for a healthy and refreshing breakfast or snack.

Nutritional Information (Per Serving): Calories: 190 | Fat: 4g | Protein: 17g | Carbohydrates: 26g | Sugars: 10g | Fiber: 6g | Sodium: 70mg.

Tacos with Scrambled Eggs

Prep Time: 10 minutes | Cook Time: 10 minutes | Serves: 2

Ingredients:

- 4 small whole wheat tortillas
- 4 large eggs
- ¼ cup low-fat milk (60ml)
- ½ cup bell peppers, diced (75g)
- ½ cup spinach, chopped (15g)
- ¼ cup low-fat shredded cheese (28g)
- Salt and pepper, to taste
- Salsa for serving (optional)

Instructions:

1. Beat the eggs with milk, salt, and pepper.
2. Spray a skillet with non-stick cooking spray and heat over medium heat.
3. Add the bell peppers and spinach, sauté for a few minutes until soft.
4. Pour the egg mixture into the skillet and scramble until cooked through.
5. Warm the tortillas in a separate pan or microwave.
6. Divide the scrambled eggs among the tortillas, top with cheese.
7. Serve with salsa if desired.

Nutritional Information (Per Serving): Calories: 315 | Fat: 15g | Protein: 18g | Carbohydrates: 30g | Sugars: 2g | Fiber: 4g | Sodium: 470mg.

Quinoa Breakfast Bowl

Prep Time: 5 minutes | Cook Time: 20 minutes | Serves: 2

Ingredients:

- ½ cup quinoa, rinsed (85g)
- 1 cup unsweetened almond milk (240ml)
- 1 tbsp sugar-free syrup or a sugar substitute (15ml)
- ½ cup mixed berries (blueberries, strawberries, raspberries) (70g)
- ¼ cup chopped nuts (almonds, walnuts) (30g)
- Pinch of cinnamon (optional)

Instructions:

1. In a small saucepan, combine quinoa and almond milk. Bring to a boil, then reduce heat to low and simmer, covered, for 15 minutes or until quinoa is cooked and liquid is absorbed.
2. Stir in the sugar-free syrup or sugar substitute and a pinch of cinnamon if desired.
3. Serve in bowls, topped with mixed berries and chopped nuts.

Nutritional Information (Per Serving): Calories: 280 | Fat: 15g | Protein: 8g | Carbohydrates: 29g | Sugars: 6g | Fiber: 5g | Sodium: 170mg.

Berry and Nut Smoothie

Prep Time: 5 minutes | Cook Time: 0 minutes | Serves: 1

Ingredients:

- ½ cup mixed berries (blueberries, raspberries, strawberries) (70g)
- 1 tbsp almonds, chopped (10g)
- 1 cup unsweetened almond milk (240ml)
- ½ scoop protein powder (optional) (15g)
- Ice cubes (optional)

Instructions:

1. In a blender, combine the mixed berries, chopped almonds, almond milk, and protein powder if using.
2. Blend on high until smooth. Add ice cubes if a thicker consistency is desired.
3. Pour into a glass and enjoy as a healthy, protein-rich breakfast or snack.

Nutritional Information (Per Serving): Calories: 210 | Fat: 9g | Protein: 10g (varies with protein powder) | Carbohydrates: 24g | Sugars: 7g | Fiber: 4g | Sodium: 200mg.

Mushroom and Spinach Frittata

Prep Time: 10 minutes | Cook Time: 15 minutes | Serves: 2

Ingredients:

- 4 large eggs
- ½ cup spinach, chopped (15g)
- ½ cup mushrooms, sliced (35g)
- ¼ cup low-fat cheese, shredded (28g)
- 1 tbsp olive oil (15ml)
- Salt and pepper, to taste

Instructions:

1. Preheat the oven to 375°F (190°C).
2. In a bowl, beat the eggs with salt and pepper.
3. Heat olive oil in an oven-safe skillet over medium heat. Sauté the mushrooms until soft.
4. Add the spinach and cook until wilted. Pour the eggs over the vegetables and sprinkle with cheese.
5. Cook for a few minutes until the edges set, then transfer to the oven.
6. Bake for 8-10 minutes or until the frittata is set and lightly golden.
7. Cut into wedges and serve.

Nutritional Information (Per Serving): Calories: 250 | Fat: 18g | Protein: 16g | Carbohydrates: 4g | Sugars: 1g | Fiber: 1g | Sodium: 370mg.

Cheese and Egg Waffles

Prep Time: 10 minutes | Cook Time: 5 minutes | Serves: 2

Ingredients:

- 4 large eggs
- 1 cup shredded cheese (such as cheddar or mozzarella) (113g)
- Salt and pepper, to taste
- Optional toppings: cooked bacon, arugula, fresh tomatoes, salad greens, thin slices of meat, poached egg, crispy spinach leaves

Instructions:

1. Preheat your waffle iron.
2. In a bowl, beat the eggs. Mix in the shredded cheese and season with salt and pepper.
3. Pour half of the egg and cheese mixture into the waffle iron, spreading evenly.
4. Close the waffle iron and cook for about 3-5 minutes or until the waffles are golden and crispy.
5. Repeat with the remaining mixture.
6. Serve the waffles hot. They can be enjoyed plain or topped with options like bacon and arugula, a salad with a slice of meat, or a poached egg with crispy spinach.

Nutritional Information (Per Serving, waffles only): Calories: 330 | Fat: 24g | Protein: 22g | Carbohydrates: 2g | Sugars: 0g | Fiber: 0g | Sodium: 620mg.

Veggie Breakfast Scramble

Prep Time: 5 minutes | Cook Time: 10 minutes | Serves: 1

Ingredients:

- 2 large eggs
- ½ cup bell peppers, diced (75g)
- ½ cup spinach, chopped (15g)
- ¼ cup onions, diced (40g)
- 1 tbsp olive oil (15ml)
- Salt and pepper to taste
- 2 tbsp low-fat cheese, shredded (optional) (14g)

Instructions:

1. Beat the eggs in a bowl, season with salt and pepper.
2. Heat olive oil in a skillet over medium heat. Add the onions and bell peppers, and sauté until soft.
3. Add the spinach and cook until wilted.
4. Pour the eggs over the vegetables and scramble until cooked through.
5. Sprinkle with cheese if using and let it melt.
6. Serve the scramble hot.

Nutritional Information (Per Serving): Calories: 270 | Fat: 20g | Protein: 15g | Carbohydrates: 9g | Sugars: 3g | Fiber: 2g | Sodium: 370mg.

Low-Carb Blueberry Muffins

Prep Time: 10 minutes | Cook Time: 20 minutes | Serves: 6

Ingredients:

- 1 ½ cups almond flour (144g)
- ½ tsp baking powder
- 3 large eggs
- 1/3 cup low-carb sweetener (67g)
- ¼ cup unsalted butter, melted (60ml)
- 1 tsp vanilla extract (5ml)
- ½ cup blueberries (72g)
- A pinch of salt

Instructions:

1. Preheat oven to 350°F (175°C). Line a muffin tin with paper liners.
2. In a bowl, whisk together almond flour, baking powder, and salt.
3. In another bowl, mix eggs, melted butter, low-carb sweetener, and vanilla extract.
4. Combine wet and dry ingredients, then gently fold in blueberries.
5. Divide the batter among the muffin cups.
6. Bake for 18-20 minutes or until a toothpick inserted into the center comes out clean.
7. Let cool before serving.

Nutritional Information (Per Serving): Calories: 287 | Fat: 25g | Protein: 8g | Carbohydrates: 8g | Sugars: 1g | Fiber: 3g | Sodium: 46mg.

Chia Seed Pudding

Prep Time: 5 minutes (plus overnight for setting) | Cook Time: 0 minutes | Serves: 2

Ingredients:

- ¼ cup chia seeds (42g)
- 1 cup unsweetened almond milk (240ml)
- 1 tbsp maple syrup or honey (optional) (15ml)
- ½ tsp vanilla extract (2.5ml)
- Toppings: Fresh berries, nuts, or coconut flakes (optional)

Instructions:

1. In a bowl, mix together chia seeds, almond milk, vanilla extract, and maple syrup or honey if using.
2. Stir well to combine and let sit for 5 minutes. Stir again to prevent clumping.
3. Cover and refrigerate overnight or for at least 6 hours.
4. Before serving, give it a good stir and add more almond milk if needed for desired consistency.
5. Top with fresh berries, nuts, or coconut flakes if desired.

Nutritional Information (Per Serving): Calories: 132 | Fat: 7g | Protein: 4g | Carbohydrates: 15g | Sugars: 5g | Fiber: 9g | Sodium: 82mg.

Homemade Caramel Granola with Coconut Flour and Berries

Prep Time: 15 minutes | Cook Time: 20-25 minutes | Serves: 6

Ingredients:

- 3 cups rolled oats (240g)
- 1 ripe banana, chopped
- 1/3 cup diabetic-friendly sweetener or sugar substitute (about 53g)
- ⅓ cup water (80ml)
- 1 tbsp vegetable oil (coconut oil recommended) (15ml)
- 2 pinches of salt
- 1 cup nuts (walnuts, almonds, or any of your choice), roughly chopped (120g)
- Optional: pumpkin or sunflower seeds, dried fruit, coconut shavings, chocolate chips for added variety

Instructions:

1. Preheat the oven to 350°F (180°C). Grease a baking sheet with coconut oil and sprinkle a pinch of coarse salt over it.
2. In a saucepan over medium heat, melt the diabetic-friendly sweetener or sugar substitute until it turns into a golden caramel, stirring occasionally. Be careful not to overheat to avoid burning.
3. Carefully add water to the caramel (it may splatter) and stir until well combined and smooth. Turn off the heat and allow the caramel to cool slightly.
4. In a large bowl, mix the rolled oats with the cooled caramel syrup. Add the chopped banana and nuts, ensuring everything is evenly coated.

5. Spread the granola mixture on the prepared baking sheet in an even layer.

6. Bake in the preheated oven for 18-25 minutes, stirring every 5 minutes to ensure even baking, until golden brown and crisp.

7. Let the granola cool completely. It will crisp up further as it cools.

8. Store the cooled granola in an airtight container.

9. Add optional ingredients like dried fruit, seeds, coconut, or chocolate as desired.

Nutritional Information (Per Serving): Calories: 330 | Fat: 13g | Protein: 8g | Carbohydrates: 35g | Sugars: 7g | Fiber: 5g | Sodium: 84mg.

Kale and White Bean Hash

Prep Time: 10 minutes | Cook Time: 15 minutes | Serves: 2

Ingredients:

- 1 cup kale, chopped (67g)
- ½ cup canned white beans, drained and rinsed (130g)
- 1 small onion, diced
- 1 clove garlic, minced
- 2 tbsp olive oil (30ml)
- 2 large eggs
- Salt and pepper to taste

Instructions:

1. Heat olive oil in a skillet over medium heat.

2. Add the onion and garlic, and sauté until translucent.

3. Add the kale and cook until it starts to wilt.

4. Stir in the white beans and cook until heated through.

5. Make two wells in the hash and crack an egg into each.

6. Cover and cook until eggs are done to your liking.

7. Season with salt and pepper and serve hot.

Nutritional Information (Per Serving): Calories: 357 | Fat: 19g | Protein: 14g | Carbohydrates: 34g | Fiber: 7g | Sugars: 2g | Sodium: 549mg

Oatmeal with Flaxseeds

Prep Time: 5 minutes | Cook Time: 5 minutes | Serves: 1

Ingredients:

- ½ cup rolled oats (40g)
- 1 cup water or unsweetened almond milk (240ml)
- 1 tbsp ground flaxseeds (7g)
- A pinch of cinnamon (optional)
- Sweetener of choice (honey, maple syrup, stevia) to taste (optional)

Instructions:

1. In a small saucepan, bring water or almond milk to a boil.

2. Add rolled oats and reduce heat to simmer. Cook for about 5 minutes, stirring occasionally, until oats are tender.

3. Remove from heat and stir in ground flaxseeds and cinnamon if using.

4. Sweeten to taste if desired.

5. Serve hot.

Nutritional Information (Per Serving): Calories: 229 | Fat: 5g | Protein: 7g | Carbohydrates: 38g | Fiber: 6g | Sugars: 0g | Sodium: 0mg

CHAPTER 4: LUNCHES: Nutritious and convenient meals for midday

Greek Avgolemono Soup

Prep time: 10 minutes | Cook Time: 20 minutes | Serves: 4

Ingredients:

- 4 cups chicken broth (960ml)
- ½ cup orzo or rice (95g)
- 2 large eggs
- Juice of 2 lemons
- 1 cup cooked, shredded chicken (140g)
- Salt and pepper to taste
- Chopped parsley for garnish

Instructions:

1. In a pot, bring chicken broth to a boil. Add orzo or rice and cook until tender.
2. In a separate bowl, whisk together the eggs and lemon juice.
3. Slowly ladle a cup of the hot broth into the egg mixture, whisking constantly to temper the eggs.
4. Gradually pour the egg mixture back into the pot, stirring continuously. Heat gently until the soup thickens slightly, but do not boil.
5. Add the cooked chicken, and season with salt, pepper and chopped parsley.

Nutritional Information (Per Serving): Calories: 230 | Fat: 8g | Protein: 18g | Carbohydrates: 20g | Fiber: 1g | Sugars: 1g | Sodium: 1013mg

Creamy Chicken, Mushroom Soup

Prep Time: 15 minutes | Cook Time: 30 minutes | Serves: 4

Ingredients:

- 2 chicken breasts, cooked and shredded (500g)
- 2 cups mushrooms, sliced (150g)
- 1 onion, diced (150g)
- 2 cloves garlic, minced (6g)
- 4 cups low-sodium chicken broth (960ml)
- 1 cup heavy cream (240ml)
- 1 tbsp olive oil (15ml)
- Salt and pepper to taste
- 1 tsp dried thyme

Instructions:

1. In a large pot, heat olive oil over medium heat. Add onions and garlic, sauté until soft.
2. Add mushrooms and thyme, cook until mushrooms are soft.
3. Pour in the chicken broth and bring to a boil.
4. Reduce heat and add shredded chicken and heavy cream. Simmer for 20 minutes.

Nutritional Information (Per Serving): Calories: 396 | Fat: 27g | Protein: 26g | Carbohydrates: 11g | Fiber: 2g | Sugars: 4g | Sodium: 272mg

Hungarian Goulash Soup

Prep time: 15 minutes | Cook Time: 1 hour | Serves: 6

Ingredients:

- 1 lb beef stew meat, cut into cubes (450g)
- 4 cups beef broth (960ml)
- 1 large onion, chopped (150g)
- 2 medium carrots, diced (120g)
- 2 medium potatoes, diced (300g)
- 2 tbsp tomato paste (30ml)
- 1 tbsp paprika
- 1 tsp caraway seeds
- Salt and pepper to taste
- Fresh parsley for garnish

Instructions:

1. In a large pot, brown the beef cubes in batches. Set aside.
2. In the same pot, sauté the onion until translucent. Add the beef back to the pot along with carrots, potatoes, tomato paste, paprika, caraway seeds, salt, and pepper.
3. Add beef broth and bring to a boil. Reduce heat and simmer for about 1 hour or until the beef is tender.
4. Adjust seasoning to taste and serve hot, garnished with fresh parsley.

Nutritional Information (Per Serving): Calories: 260 | Fat: 9g | Protein: 20g | Carbohydrates: 23g | Fiber: 4g | Sugars: 5g | Sodium: 953mg

Chicken Dumpling Soup

Prep Time: 20 minutes | Cook Time: 30 minutes | Serves: 4

Ingredients:

- 4 cups chicken broth (960ml)
- 2 cups water (480ml)
- 2 medium carrots, chopped (120g)
- 2 celery stalks, chopped (80g)
- 1 small onion, diced (70g)
- 2 tsp baking powder
- 1 lb chicken breast, cut into small pieces (450g)
- 1 cup all-purpose flour (120g)
- ½ tsp salt
- ½ cup milk (120ml)
- Fresh parsley for garnish
- Salt and pepper to taste

Instructions:

1. In a large pot, combine chicken broth, water, carrots, celery, onion, and chicken pieces. Bring to a boil, then reduce heat and simmer for 20 minutes.
2. In a bowl, mix flour, baking powder, and salt. Stir in milk to form a dough.
3. Drop spoonfuls of dough into the simmering soup. Cover and cook for 10 minutes without lifting the lid.
4. Season the soup with salt and pepper to taste.
5. Garnish with fresh parsley and serve hot.

Nutritional Information (Per Serving): Calories: 225 | Fat: 3g | Protein: 22g | Carbohydrates: 29g | Fiber: 2g | Sugars: 3g | Sodium: 1416mg

Beef Medallions with Mustard Sauce

Prep Time: 15 minutes | Cook Time: 20 minutes | Serves: 2

Ingredients:

- 4 beef medallions (1 lb) (450g)
- 1 tbsp olive oil (15ml)
- 1/4 cup low-fat cream (60ml)
- 1 tbsp Dijon mustard (15ml)
- 1 tsp Worcestershire sauce (5ml)
- Salt and pepper to taste

Instructions:

1. Season the beef medallions with salt and pepper.
2. Heat olive oil in a skillet over medium-high heat.
3. Add beef and cook to desired doneness, about 4–5 minutes per side for medium-rare. Remove and keep warm.
4. In the same skillet, add cream, mustard, and Worcestershire sauce. Cook while stirring for a few minutes until thickened.
5. Return the beef medallions to the pan and coat with the mustard sauce.
6. Serve the medallions with sauce drizzled over the top.

Nutritional Information (Per Serving): Calories: 340 | Fat: 21g | Protein: 30g | Carbohydrates: 2g | Fiber: 0g | Sugars: 1g | Sodium: 330mg

Beef Rolls with Cheese and Asparagus

Prep Time: 20 minutes | Cook Time: 20 minutes | Serves: 4

Ingredients:

- 8 thin slices of beef (1 lb) (450g)
- 16 asparagus spears, trimmed
- 1 cup low-fat cheese, grated (100g)
- Salt and pepper to taste
- 1 tbsp olive oil (15ml)

Instructions:

1. Preheat the oven to 375°F (190°C).
2. Season beef slices with salt and pepper. Place two asparagus spears and a sprinkle of cheese on each slice.
3. Roll up the slices tightly and secure with toothpicks.
4. Heat olive oil in a skillet over medium-high heat. Brown the beef rolls on all sides.
5. Transfer the rolls to a baking dish and bake in the oven for 10–15 minutes, or until cooked to desired doneness.
6. Serve the beef rolls hot, with any pan juices drizzled over the top.

Nutritional Information (Per Serving): Calories: 335 | Fat: 20g | Protein: 33g | Carbohydrates: 3g | Fiber: 1g | Sugars: 1g | Sodium: 380mg

Pork with Mushrooms and Bell Peppers in Cream Sauce

Prep Time: 15 minutes | Cook Time: 20 minutes | Serves: 4

Ingredients:

- 1 lb pork tenderloin, sliced into medallions (450g)
- 1 cup mushrooms, sliced (70g)
- 1 bell pepper, sliced (150g)
- 1 cup low-fat cream (240ml)
- 1 tbsp olive oil (15ml)
- 1 clove garlic, minced
- Salt and pepper to taste
- Fresh parsley, chopped for garnish

Instructions:

1. Season pork medallions with salt and pepper.
2. Heat olive oil in a skillet over medium-high heat.
3. Add pork and cook until browned on both sides.
4. Remove from skillet and set aside.
5. In the same skillet, add garlic, mushrooms, and bell pepper. Sauté until vegetables are tender.
6. Lower the heat, add the cream, and stir to combine. Return pork to the skillet and simmer for 5-7 minutes.
7. Adjust seasoning with salt and pepper. Garnish with fresh parsley before serving.

Nutritional Information (Per Serving): Calories: 318 | Fat: 20g | Protein: 26g | Carbohydrates: 9g | Fiber: 2g | Sugars: 4g | Sodium: 87mg

Herb-Crusted Pork with Roasted Zucchini

Prep Time: 15 minutes | Cook Time: 25 minutes | Serves: 4

Ingredients:

- 1 lb pork tenderloin (450g)
- 2 tbsp mixed dried herbs (such as rosemary, thyme, oregano)
- 2 zucchinis, sliced (500g)
- 1 tbsp olive oil (15ml)
- Salt and pepper to taste

Instructions:

1. Preheat the oven to 375°F (190°C).
2. Rub the pork with olive oil, salt, pepper, and mixed herbs.
3. Place the pork in a roasting pan. Surround with sliced zucchini. Drizzle zucchini with a little olive oil and season with salt and pepper.
4. Roast in the oven for 25 minutes or until the pork reaches an internal temperature of 145°F (63°C).
5. Let the pork rest for a few minutes before slicing.
6. Serve with roasted zucchini.

Nutritional Information (Per Serving): Calories: 226 | Fat: 8g | Protein: 27g | Carbohydrates: 13g | Fiber: 4g | Sugars: 6g | Sodium: 77mg

Warm Pork and Vegetable Salad

Prep Time: 15 minutes | Cook Time: 20 minutes | Serves: 4

Ingredients:

- 1 lb pork loin, thinly sliced (450g)
- 2 cups mixed salad greens (60g)
- 1 cup cherry tomatoes, halved (150g)
- 1 cucumber, sliced (200g)
- 1 red bell pepper, sliced (150g)
- 2 tbsp balsamic vinegar (30ml)
- 1 tbsp olive oil (15ml)
- Salt and pepper to taste

Instructions:

1. Season the pork slices with salt and pepper.
2. Heat olive oil in a skillet over medium-high heat. Add pork and cook until browned and cooked through.
3. In a large bowl, combine salad greens, cherry tomatoes, cucumber, and red bell pepper.
4. Add the warm pork to the salad. Drizzle with balsamic vinegar and toss gently to combine.
5. Serve the salad warm.

Nutritional Information (Per Serving): Calories: 243 | Fat: 11g | Protein: 24g | Carbohydrates: 11g | Fiber: 2g | Sugars: 5g | Sodium: 51mg

Mushroom Soup with Cheese

Prep Time: 10 minutes | Cook Time: 20 minutes | Serves: 4

Ingredients:

- 4 cups mushrooms, sliced (300g)
- 1 onion, diced (150g)
- 2 cloves garlic, minced (6g)
- 4 cups low-sodium chicken or vegetable broth (960ml)
- 1 cup low-fat milk (240ml)
- ½ cup grated low-fat cheese (50g)
- 2 tbsp olive oil (30ml)
- Salt and pepper to taste
- Fresh parsley, chopped for garnish

Instructions:

1. Heat olive oil in a large pot over medium heat. Sauté onion and garlic until translucent.
2. Add mushrooms and cook until they are soft and browned.
3. Pour in the broth and bring to a simmer. Cook for 10 minutes.
4. Add milk and cheese to the pot. Stir until the cheese is melted and the soup is heated through.
5. Season with salt and pepper to taste.
6. Serve hot, garnished with fresh parsley.

Nutritional Information (Per Serving): Calories: 151 | Fat: 8g | Protein: 8g | Carbohydrates: 13g | Fiber: 2g | Sugars: 7g | Sodium: 251mg

Braised Beef with Vegetables and Thyme

Prep Time: 15 minutes | Cook Time: 2 hours | Serves: 6

Ingredients:

- 2 lbs beef chuck, cut into chunks (907g)
- 4 cups beef broth (960ml)
- 2 carrots, chopped (approximately 130g each)
- 2 potatoes, chopped (approximately 300g each)
- 1 onion, chopped (approximately 150g)
- 2 cloves garlic, minced (6g)
- 2 tsp dried thyme
- 1 tbsp olive oil (15ml)
- Salt and pepper to taste

Instructions:

1. Season beef with salt and pepper. In a large pot, heat olive oil over medium-high heat and brown the beef on all sides.
2. Add onions and garlic to the pot and sauté until softened.
3. Add broth, carrots, potatoes, and thyme. Bring to a boil, then reduce heat to low. Cover and simmer for about 2 hours or until beef is tender.
4. Adjust seasoning with salt and pepper.
5. Serve the braised beef and vegetables hot.

Nutritional Information (Per Serving): Calories: 402 | Fat: 16g | Protein: 40g | Carbohydrates: 24g | Fiber: 4g | Sugars: 3g | Sodium: 656mg

Beef and Vegetable Minestrone

Prep Time: 15 minutes | Cook Time: 30 minutes | Serves: 6

Ingredients:

- 1 lb lean ground beef (450g)
- 4 cups low-sodium beef broth (960ml)
- 1 can (14.5 oz) diced tomatoes (411g)
- 1 cup carrots, diced (130g)
- 1 cup celery, diced (100g)
- 1 cup zucchini, diced (120g)
- 1 onion, chopped (150g)
- 2 cloves garlic, minced (6g)
- 1 cup small pasta, like ditalini or elbow macaroni (100g)
- 2 tsp Italian seasoning
- Salt and pepper to taste
- Fresh parsley, chopped for garnish

Instructions:

1. In a large pot, cook the ground beef over medium heat until browned. Drain excess fat.
2. Add onions and garlic to the pot and sauté until softened.
3. Add broth, tomatoes, carrots, celery, zucchini, Italian seasoning, salt, and pepper. Bring to a boil.
4. Add pasta and simmer for about 10 minutes or until pasta is tender.
5. Adjust seasoning to taste.
6. Serve hot, garnished with fresh parsley.

Nutritional Information (Per Serving): Calories: 289 | Fat: 8g | Protein: 18g | Carbohydrates: 35g | Fiber: 5g | Sugars: 7g | Sodium: 583mg

Chicken Piccata with Capers

Prep Time: 15 minutes | Cook Time: 20 minutes | Serves: 4

Ingredients:

- 4 boneless, skinless chicken breast halves (about 1 lb) (450g)
- ¼ cup all-purpose flour (31g)
- 2 tbsp olive oil (30ml)
- ½ cup low-sodium chicken broth (120ml)
- Juice of 1 lemon
- 2 tbsp capers, drained
- Salt and pepper to taste
- Fresh parsley, chopped for garnish

Instructions:

1. Season chicken breasts with salt and pepper. Dredge in flour, shaking off excess.
2. Heat olive oil in a skillet over medium-high heat.
3. Cook chicken until golden and cooked through, about 4-5 minutes per side. Remove from skillet and set aside.
4. In the same skillet, add chicken broth and lemon juice, scraping up any browned bits. Simmer until slightly reduced.
5. Return chicken to the skillet. Add capers and simmer for 2-3 minutes.
6. Serve chicken with sauce, garnished with fresh parsley.

Nutritional Information (Per Serving): Calories: 234 | Fat: 10g | Protein: 26g | Carbohydrates: 8g | Fiber: 1g | Sugars: 0g | Sodium: 428mg

Herbed Turkey and Quinoa Stuffed Bell Peppers

Prep Time: 20 minutes | Cook Time: 40 minutes | Serves: 4

Ingredients:

- 4 large bell peppers, tops cut off and seeds removed
- 1 lb ground turkey (450g)
- 1 cup cooked quinoa (185g)
- 1 small onion, diced (70g)
- 1 clove garlic, minced (3g)
- 1 tsp dried Italian herbs
- 1 cup low-sodium tomato sauce (240ml)
- 2 tbsp olive oil (30ml)
- Salt and pepper to taste

Instructions:

1. Preheat oven to 375°F (190°C).
2. Heat 1 tablespoon olive oil in a skillet over medium heat. Add turkey, onion, garlic, herbs, salt, and pepper. Cook until turkey is browned.
3. Remove from heat. Mix in cooked quinoa and half of the tomato sauce.
4. Stuff bell peppers with turkey and quinoa mixture. Place in a baking dish.
5. Top each pepper with remaining tomato sauce. Drizzle with remaining olive oil.
6. Cover with foil and bake for 30–40 minutes until peppers are tender.

Nutritional Information (Per Serving): Calories: 331 | Fat: 12g | Protein: 24g | Carbohydrates: 34g | Fiber: 5g | Sugars: 7g | Sodium: 517mg

Lamb Meatballs with Tzatziki Sauce

Prep Time: 20 minutes | Cook Time: 20 minutes | Serves: 4

Ingredients:

For Meatballs:

- 1 lb ground lamb (450g)
- 1 small onion, grated (70g)
- 2 cloves garlic, minced (6g)
- 1 tsp cumin
- 1 tsp paprika
- Salt and pepper to taste

For Tzatziki Sauce:

- 1 cup Greek yogurt (245g)
- 1 cucumber, seeded and grated (approximately 150g)
- 2 tbsp lemon juice (30ml)
- 1 clove garlic, minced (3g)
- 1 tbsp fresh dill, chopped
- Salt and pepper to taste

Instructions:

1. Preheat oven to 375°F (190°C).
2. In a bowl, mix together lamb, onion, garlic, cumin, paprika, salt, and pepper. Form into small meatballs.
3. Place meatballs on a baking sheet and bake for 20 minutes or until cooked through.
4. For the sauce, combine Greek yogurt, cucumber, lemon juice, garlic, dill, salt, and pepper in a bowl.
5. Serve meatballs with tzatziki sauce on the side.

Nutritional Information (Per Serving): Calories: 385 | Fat: 28g | Protein: 23g | Carbohydrates: 12g | Fiber: 2g | Sugars: 5g | Sodium: 276mg

Spiced Duck Breast with Orange Glaze

Prep Time: 15 minutes | Cook Time: 25 minutes | Serves: 2

Ingredients:

- 2 duck breasts
- 1 tsp ground coriander
- 1 tsp ground cumin
- Salt and pepper to taste
- 1 tsp grated ginger
- ½ cup freshly squeezed orange juice (no added sugar) (120ml)
- 2 tbsp honey (or a sugar-free sweetener) (30ml)

Instructions:

1. Score the skin of the duck breasts and season with coriander, cumin, salt, and pepper.
2. Heat a skillet over medium heat. Place duck breasts skin-side down and cook for about 6-8 minutes until the skin is crisp. Flip and cook for another 5-7 minutes for medium-rare. Remove and let rest.
3. In the same skillet, add freshly squeezed orange juice and honey (or a sugar-free sweetener) along with grated ginger if desired. Simmer until the sauce thickens into a glaze.
4. Slice the duck and serve with the orange glaze.

Nutritional Information (Per Serving): Calories: 385 | Fat: 28g | Protein: 23g | Carbohydrates: 12g | Fiber: 0.5g | Sugars: 10g | Sodium: 95mg

Spiced Lamb Skewers with Greek Yogurt Dip

Prep Time: 20 minutes (plus marinating time) | Cook Time: 10 minutes | Serves: 4

Ingredients:

For Lamb Skewers:

- 1 lb lamb, cut into chunks (450g)
- 1 tsp paprika
- 1 tsp ground cumin
- 1 clove garlic, minced (3g)
- Salt and pepper to taste
- Wooden or metal skewers

For Greek Yogurt Dip:

- 1 cup Greek yogurt (245g)
- 1 tbsp lemon juice (15ml)
- 1 tbsp chopped fresh mint
- Salt and pepper to taste

Instructions:

1. Mix lamb with paprika, cumin, garlic, salt, and pepper. Marinate for at least 1 hour.
2. Thread the lamb chunks onto skewers.
3. Preheat grill or grill pan to medium-high. Grill skewers, turning occasionally, until cooked to desired doneness, about 6-8 minutes.
4. For the dip, mix Greek yogurt with lemon juice, mint, salt, and pepper.
5. Serve lamb skewers with Greek yogurt dip.

Nutritional Information (Per Serving): Calories: 314 | Fat: 15g | Carbohydrates: 6g | Protein: 38g | Fiber: 1g | Sugars: 3g | Sodium: 105mg

Buckwheat Patties with Cheese and Mushrooms

Prep Time: 15 minutes | Cook Time: 15 minutes | Serves: 4

Ingredients:

- 2 cups cooked buckwheat (340g)
- 1 cup grated cheese (low-fat option) (100g)
- 1 cup mushrooms, finely chopped (70g)
- 1 small onion, finely chopped (70g)
- 2 eggs
- Salt and pepper to taste
- 2 tbsp olive oil for cooking (30ml)

Instructions:

1. In a large bowl, combine cooked buckwheat, cheese, mushrooms, onion, eggs, salt, and pepper. Mix well.
2. Form the mixture into patties.
3. Heat olive oil in a skillet over medium heat. Cook patties for about 3-4 minutes on each side or until golden brown and cooked through.
4. Serve hot.

Nutritional Information (Per Serving): Calories: 285 | Fat: 15g | Carbohydrates: 27g | Fiber: 4g | Sugars: 1g | Protein: 13g | Sodium: 180mg

Baked Chicken Breast with Tomatoes and Mozzarella

Chicken Legs in Keto Honey Sauce

Prep Time: 10 minutes | Cook Time: 25 minutes | Serves: 4

Prep Time: 15 minutes | Cook Time: 30 minutes | Serves: 4

Ingredients:

Ingredients:

- 4 boneless, skinless chicken breasts
- 2 tomatoes, sliced
- 1 cup shredded low-fat mozzarella cheese (100g)
- 1 tbsp Italian seasoning
- Salt and pepper to taste
- 1 tbsp olive oil (15ml)

- 8 chicken legs
- 1/4 cup keto-friendly honey alternative (60ml)
- 2 tbsp apple cider vinegar (30ml)
- 1 tbsp soy sauce (low sodium) (15ml)
- 2 cloves garlic, minced (6g)
- 1 tsp ground ginger
- Salt and pepper to taste
- 1 tbsp olive oil (15ml)

Instructions:

1. Preheat the oven to 375°F (190°C).
Season chicken breasts with salt, pepper, and Italian seasoning.
2. In a baking dish, place the chicken and top each breast with tomato slices and mozzarella cheese.
3. Drizzle with olive oil.
4. Bake for 25 minutes, or until the chicken is cooked through and the cheese is melted and slightly browned.

Instructions:

1. Preheat the oven to 375°F (190°C).
2. In a bowl, mix the keto honey alternative, apple cider vinegar, soy sauce, garlic, and ginger. Season with salt and pepper.
3. Toss the chicken legs in the mixture until well coated.
4. Arrange the chicken legs on a baking tray and drizzle with olive oil.
5. Bake for 30 minutes, turning halfway through, until the chicken is cooked and the sauce is caramelized.

Nutritional Information (Per Serving): Calories: 290 | Fat: 11g | Carbohydrates: 4g | Fiber: 1g | Sugars: 2g | Protein: 42g | Sodium: 340mg

Nutritional Information (Per Serving): Calories: 370 | Fat: 23g | Carbohydrates: 5g | Fiber: 0g | Sugars: 1g | Protein: 36g | Sodium: 290mg

Chicken Drumsticks with Spicy Chimichurri Sauce

Prep Time: 20 minutes | Cook Time: 25 minutes | Serves: 4

Ingredients:

- 8 chicken drumsticks
- 1 cup fresh parsley (60g)
- 1/2 cup olive oil (120ml)
- 2 tbsp red wine vinegar (30ml)
- 2 cloves garlic (approximately 6g)
- 1 tsp red pepper flakes
- Salt and pepper to taste

Instructions:

1. Preheat the oven to 375°F (190°C).
2. Season the chicken drumsticks with salt and pepper.
3. Bake the drumsticks for 25 minutes, or until fully cooked.
4. Meanwhile, blend parsley, olive oil, red wine vinegar, garlic, and red pepper flakes to make the chimichurri sauce.
5. Serve the baked drumsticks with the spicy chimichurri sauce on the side.

Nutritional Information (Per Serving): Calories: 419 | Fat: 34g | Carbohydrates: 3g | Fiber: 1g | Sugars: 0g | Protein: 25g | Sodium: 120mg

Chicken Soup with Cauliflower and Thyme

Prep Time: 10 minutes | Cook Time: 35 minutes | Serves: 4

Ingredients:

- 4 cups chicken broth (low sodium) (960ml)
- 2 cups cauliflower florets (200g)
- 1 cup shredded cooked chicken (140g)
- 1 onion, chopped (150g)
- 2 carrots, sliced (120g each)
- 2 celery stalks, sliced (40g each)
- 2 cloves garlic, minced (6g)
- 1 tsp fresh thyme
- Salt and pepper to taste
- 1 tbsp olive oil (15ml)

Instructions:

1. In a large pot, heat olive oil over medium heat.
2. Add onion, carrots, celery, and garlic. Cook until softened.
3. Add chicken broth, cauliflower, and thyme. Bring to a boil.
4. Reduce heat and simmer for 25 minutes.
5. Add the shredded chicken and cook for an additional 10 minutes.
6. Season with salt and pepper before serving.

Nutritional Information (Per Serving): Calories: 144 | Fat: 5g | Carbohydrates: 10g | Fiber: 3g | Sugars: 4g | Protein: 14g | Sodium: 860mg

Chicken, Avocado, and Walnut Salad

Prep Time: 15 minutes | Cook Time: 0 minutes | Serves: 4

Ingredients:

- 2 cups cooked chicken, shredded (280g)
- 2 avocados, diced (approximately 450g total)
- 1/2 cup walnuts, chopped (50g)
- 4 cups mixed salad greens (approximately 120g)
- 1/4 cup olive oil (60ml)
- Juice of 1 lemon (45ml)
- Salt and pepper to taste

Instructions:

1. In a large bowl, combine shredded chicken, avocado, and walnuts.
2. In a small bowl, whisk together olive oil, lemon juice, salt, and pepper to make the dressing.
3. Toss the salad greens with the dressing, then add the chicken mixture.
4. Serve immediately.

Nutritional Information (Per Serving): Calories: 469 | Fat: 39g | Carbohydrates: 13g | Fiber: 9g | Sugars: 2g | Protein: 19g | Sodium: 103mg

Asian Beef Salad with Sesame Dressing

Prep Time: 15 minutes | Cook Time: 10 minutes | Serves: 4

Ingredients:

- 1 lb lean beef steak, thinly sliced (450g)
- 4 cups mixed salad greens (approximately 120g)
- 1 red bell pepper, thinly sliced (approximately 150g)
- 1 carrot, julienned (approximately 61g)
- 1/4 cup cilantro leaves
- 2 tbsp sesame oil (30ml)
- 1 tbsp soy sauce (low sodium) (15ml)
- 1 tbsp rice vinegar (15ml)
- 1 tsp honey (5ml)
- 1 tsp grated ginger
- Sesame seeds for garnish

Instructions:

1. Whisk together sesame oil, soy sauce, rice vinegar, honey, and ginger to make the dressing.
2. In a pan, cook the beef slices over medium heat until just cooked, about 2-3 minutes per side.
3. In a large bowl, combine salad greens, bell pepper, and carrot.
4. Add cooked beef to the salad and toss with the dressing.
5. Garnish with cilantro and sesame seeds.

Nutritional Information (Per Serving): Calories: 336 | Fat: 18g | Carbohydrates: 10g | Fiber: 3g | Sugars: 5g | Protein: 32g | Sodium: 420mg

Buckwheat-Stuffed Chicken

Prep Time: 1 hour (including marination) | Cook Time: 1 hour | Serves: 4-6

Ingredients:

- 1 whole chicken (about 4.4 lbs) (2000g)
- ¾ cup buckwheat groats (135g)
- 5 oz mushrooms, sliced (140g)
- 1 medium onion, chopped (150g)
- 6 cloves garlic, minced (18g)
- 4 tbsp vegetable oil (60ml)
- Salt and black pepper to taste
- Optional: assorted vegetables (like zucchini and bell pepper) for a side dish

Instructions:

1. Rinse the buckwheat and cover with boiling water (about 1 ¼ cups), let it soak.
2. Remove the breastbone from the chicken to create more space for stuffing. Rinse the chicken and rub inside and outside with minced garlic, salt, and pepper. Let it marinate for an hour.
3. In a skillet, heat 2 tbsp of oil and sauté the onion until golden. Add mushrooms and cook until reduced in size. Drain the buckwheat and add to the skillet. Season with salt and pepper. This is your stuffing.
4. Preheat the oven to 356°F (180°C).
5. Fill the chicken cavity with the buckwheat stuffing, secure the opening with toothpicks.
6. Place the chicken in a baking dish, drizzle with the remaining oil, and roast for about 1 hour, or until the chicken is cooked through and golden.
7. Optionally, 20 minutes before the end of cooking, add assorted vegetables to the baking dish.
8. Serve the chicken with the roasted vegetables, drizzled with the cooking juices.

Nutritional Information (Per Serving): Calories: 539 | Fat: 26g | Carbohydrates: 35g | Fiber: 5g | Sugars: 2g | Protein: 40g | Sodium: 108mg

Vegan Banana Toffee

Prep Time: 15 minutes | Freeze Time: 30-50 minutes | Serves: 6

Ingredients:

- 1 ripe or overripe banana
- 2 tbsp unsweetened cocoa powder
- 3.5 tbsp coconut oil
- 1/2 tbsp peanut butter (7.5ml)
- 1/4 cup peanuts (30g)
- (Alternative: use sugar-free dark chocolate, 70% or more, instead of cocoa powder and coconut oil)

Instructions:

1. Melt the coconut oil (heat to at least 77°F, 25°C).
2. Combine banana, cocoa powder, melted coconut oil, and peanut butter (if using) in a blender. Blend until smooth.
3. Pour the mixture into a silicone mold, preferably with portioned cells.
4. Optionally, add peanuts or walnuts, gently pressing them into the mixture.
5. Freeze for 30–50 minutes. Once set, remove from the mold and cut into cubes.
6. Store in the freezer.

Nutritional Information (Per Serving): Calories: 102 | Fat: 10g | Carbohydrates: 3g | Fiber: 1g | Sugars: 1g | Protein: 1g | Sodium: 1mg

Stevia-Sweetened Lemon Tart

Prep Time: 20 minutes | Cook Time: 25 minutes | Serves: 8

Ingredients:

- 1 cup almond flour (96g)
- 1/4 cup butter, melted (60ml)
- 3 eggs
- 1/2 cup lemon juice (120ml)
- Zest of 2 lemons
- 1/3 cup stevia or another sugar substitute
- 1/2 tsp vanilla extract

Instructions:

1. Preheat the oven to 350°F (175°C). Mix almond flour and melted butter, press into the bottom of a tart pan.
2. In a bowl, whisk together eggs, lemon juice, lemon zest, stevia, and vanilla extract.
3. Pour the lemon mixture over the crust and bake for 25 minutes or until set.

Nutritional Information (Per Serving): Calories: 195 | Fat: 17g | Carbohydrates: 5g | Fiber: 1g | Sugars: 1g | Protein: 5g | Sodium: 65mg

Avocado and Blueberry Trifle

Prep Time: 25 minutes | Serves: 2

Ingredients:

- 1 ripe avocado (113g)
- 2/3 cup coconut milk (160ml)
- 1/2 cup blueberries (75g)
- 1/4 cup pecan nuts (30g)
- 1 tbsp lemon juice (15ml)
- Fresh herbs for garnish (optional)
- (Alternative: Use coconut cream instead of coconut milk for a creamier texture)

Instructions:

1. In a blender, pour in coconut milk and add the ripe avocado flesh along with lemon juice. Blend until smooth and creamy. For added flavor, consider mixing in a bit of cinnamon, vanilla extract, or ground coffee.
2. In a separate bowl, prepare the blueberries. Mash them with a fork or blend slightly for a smoother texture. You can also use raspberries, strawberries, or blackberries as alternatives.
3. To assemble, take two small jars or cups. Layer the bottom with half of the avocado and coconut mixture.
4. Add half of the mashed blueberries over the avocado layer.

5. Repeat with another layer of the avocado mixture and top with the remaining blueberries.
6. Garnish with broken pecan nuts and a few green leaves (like pea shoots) for decoration.

Nutritional Information (Per Serving): Calories: 160 | Fat: 33g | Carbohydrates: 20g | Fiber: 9g | Sugars: 7g | Protein: 4g | Sodium: 20mg

Low-Calorie Chocolate Mousse with Chicory and Raspberry

Prep Time: 15 minutes | Chill Time: 2 hours | Serves: 4

Ingredients:

- 1 cup silken tofu (262g)
- 1/4 cup unsweetened cocoa powder (21g)
- 1 tsp vanilla extract (5ml)
- 2 tbsp chicory root syrup (30ml)
- 1/2 cup fresh raspberries (61g)

Instructions:

1. lend silken tofu, cocoa powder, chicory root syrup, and vanilla extract in a blender until smooth.
2. Divide the mixture into serving cups and refrigerate for at least 2 hours.
3. Top with fresh raspberries before serving.

Nutritional Information (Per Serving): Calories: 180 | Fat: 3g | Carbohydrates: 11g | Fiber: 4g | Sugars: 4g | Protein: 4g | Sodium: 27mg

Chia Pudding with Avocado

Prep Time: 15 minutes | Chill Time: 2 hours | Serves: 2

Ingredients:

- 1 ripe avocado (100g)
- 1/3 cup coconut milk (80ml)
- 2 tsp honey (or sugar substitute) (10ml)
- Juice and zest of half a lemon (22.5ml juice)
- 1 tbsp chopped pistachios (15g)
- 2 tbsp chia seeds (28g)

Instructions:

1. Scoop out the avocado flesh and place it in a blender.
2. Add coconut milk, chia seeds, honey, and lemon juice and zest to the blender.
3. Blend until the mixture is smooth and creamy.
4. Pour the mixture into a bowl or divide it into serving glasses.
5. Refrigerate for at least 2 hours, allowing the chia seeds to swell and the pudding to set.
6. Before serving, garnish with chopped pistachios for a crunchy texture.

Nutritional Information (Per Serving): Calories: Approx. 200 | Fat: 23g | Carbohydrates: 19g | Fiber: 10g | Sugars: 7g | Protein: 4g | Sodium: 19mg

Coconut Flour Brownies

Prep Time: 20 minutes | Cook Time: 25 minutes | Serves: 9

Ingredients:

- 1/2 cup unsweetened cocoa powder (43g)
- 1/3 cup butter, melted (or coconut oil for dairy-free) (76g)
- 6 large eggs, room temperature
- 1/3 cup xylitol or sugar substitute (67g)
- 1/2 cup coconut flour (56g)
- 3 oz sugar-free dark chocolate, chopped (85g)
- 1/4 tsp salt

Instructions:

1. Preheat the oven to 350°F (175°C). Line a 8x8 inch baking pan with parchment paper or lightly grease it.
2. In a bowl, mix melted butter and cocoa powder until smooth and free of lumps.
3. Add eggs, xylitol (or sugar substitute), and salt to the cocoa mixture. Stir until well combined.
4. Gradually mix in coconut flour until the batter is uniform.
5. Fold in the chopped sugar-free dark chocolate.
6. Pour the batter into the prepared pan, spreading evenly.
7. Bake in the preheated oven for about 25 minutes. The brownies are done when the top is set and a toothpick inserted comes out mostly clean.

8. Cool completely in the pan, then cut into squares.

Nutritional Information (Per Serving): Calories: 163 | Fat: 15g | Carbohydrates: 8g | Fiber: 4g | Sugars: 1g | Protein: 6g | Sodium: 98mg

Sugar-Free Apple Mousse

Prep Time: 15 minutes | Chill Time: 1 hour | Serves: 4

Ingredients:

- 2 large apples, peeled and diced
- 1/2 cup water (120ml)
- 1 tsp cinnamon
- 1/2 tsp nutmeg
- 1/4 cup heavy cream or coconut cream (60ml)
- Sugar substitute to taste (optional)

Instructions:

1. In a saucepan, combine apples, water, cinnamon, and nutmeg. Cook over medium heat until apples are soft.
2. Blend the cooked apple mixture until smooth. Add sugar substitute if desired.
3. In a separate bowl, whip the cream until it forms soft peaks.
4. Gently fold the whipped cream into the apple mixture.
5. Divide into serving dishes and refrigerate for at least 1 hour before serving.

Nutritional Information (Per Serving): Calories: 140 | Fat: 7g | Carbohydrates: 13g | Fiber: 3g | Sugars: 8g | Protein: 1g | Sodium: 7mg

Keto Dark Chocolate Truffles

Prep Time: 20 minutes | Chill Time: 1 hour | Serves: 10

Ingredients:

- 1 cup unsweetened dark chocolate chips (sugar-free) (175g)
- 1/2 cup heavy cream (120ml)
- 1 tbsp low-carb sweetener (15g)
- 1 tsp vanilla extract (5ml)
- Unsweetened cocoa powder for dusting

Instructions:

1. In a saucepan, heat heavy cream and low-carb sweetener until just simmering. Do not boil.
2. Pour the hot cream over the dark chocolate chips and let sit for 1 minute, then stir until smooth.
3. Add vanilla extract and stir again. Let the mixture cool to room temperature.
4. Refrigerate the mixture until it's firm enough to shape, about 1 hour.
5. Scoop and roll the mixture into small balls, then dust with cocoa powder.

Nutritional Information (Per Serving): Calories: 160 | Fat: 11g | Carbohydrates: 8g | Fiber: 2g | Sugars: 0g | Protein: 1g | Sodium: 4mg

Almond Flour Chocolate Chip Cookies

Prep Time: 15 minutes | Cook Time: 10 minutes | Serves: 12

Ingredients:

- 2 cups almond flour (192g)
- 1/2 cup low-carb sweetener (100g)
- 1/2 cup butter, softened (113g)
- 1 tsp vanilla extract (5ml)
- 1/2 cup sugar-free chocolate chips (85g)
- 1 egg
- 1/2 tsp baking soda
- Pinch of salt

Instructions:

1. Preheat the oven to 350°F (175°C).
2. In a bowl, mix butter, sugar substitute, and vanilla extract. Add the egg and mix well.
3. Stir in almond flour, baking soda, and salt. Fold in chocolate chips.
4. Drop spoonfuls of dough on a baking sheet lined with parchment paper.
5. Bake for 10 minutes or until golden. Let cool before serving.

Nutritional Information (Per Serving): Calories: 228 | Fat: 20g | Carbohydrates: 7g | Fiber: 2g | Sugars: 1g | Protein: 5g | Sodium: 124mg

Healthy Chocolate Banana Candies

Prep Time: 20 minutes | Chill Time: 2 hours (optional) | Serves: 6

Ingredients:

- 5 crispbreads (like rice cakes or unsalted multigrain crispbreads)
- 1 ripe banana
- 3 tbsp unsweetened cocoa powder (15g)
- 4 tbsp unsweetened cornflakes (12g)
- Optional: 4-6 dates or dried apricots (soaked if dry) for added sweetness

Instructions:

1. Crush the crispbreads into fine crumbs and combine with the banana in a mixing bowl. Blend using a food processor or mash well with a fork until smooth.
2. Add cocoa powder (and soaked dates or apricots if using) to the banana mixture and mix until it forms a thick, dough-like consistency. Adjust the thickness by adding more crushed crispbreads or cocoa powder if necessary.
3. Crush the cornflakes into small pieces, but not into powder, for coating the candies.
4. Moisten your hands with water and form the banana mixture into small, walnut-sized balls.
5. Roll each candy ball in the crushed cornflakes to coat.
6. Refrigerate the candies for 2 hours to firm up.

7. Store the candies in the refrigerator for up to 2 days.

Nutritional Information (Per Serving): Calories: 69 | Fat: 1g | Carbohydrates: 15g | Fiber: 2g | Sugars: 5g | Protein: 2g | Sodium: 45mg

Cinnamon Spiced Baked Pears

Prep Time: 10 minutes | Cook Time: 30 minutes | Serves: 4

Ingredients:

- 2 large pears, halved and cored
- 2 tbsp butter, melted (30ml)
- 1 tsp cinnamon
- A pinch of nutmeg
- Optional: Sugar substitute to taste

Instructions:

1. Preheat the oven to 350°F (175°C).
2. Place pear halves on a baking sheet.
3. Brush each pear half with melted butter, then sprinkle with cinnamon, nutmeg, and sugar substitute if using.
4. Bake for 30 minutes or until pears are tender.

Nutritional Information (Per Serving): Calories: 150 | Fat: 5g | Carbohydrates: 13g | Fiber: 3g | Sugars: 7g | Protein: 1g | Sodium: 34mg

Healthy Peanut Butter Baskets

Prep Time: 20 minutes | Cook Time: 10 minutes | Serves: 6

Ingredients:

- 1 cup oat flour
- 2 tbsp peanut butter
- 1/4 cup water (60ml)
- Sugar substitute equivalent to 2.5 tbsp sugar
- 1 1/2 cups milk (or a non-dairy alternative) (360ml)
- 1 egg yolk
- 3 tbsp cornstarch (27g)
- 1 packet vanilla sugar (or 1 tsp vanilla extract with a sugar substitute)
- 3 tsp unsweetened cocoa powder
- 1 tsp instant coffee
- 1/4 cup peanuts, chopped (can substitute with hazelnuts or walnuts) (30g)
- Dark chocolate for garnish (optional)

Instructions:

1. Preheat the oven to 350°F (175°C).
2. To make the baskets, mix oat flour, peanut butter, water, and sugar substitute to form a dough. Adjust the water as needed for consistency.
3. Press the dough into silicone muffin cups, making small baskets. Prick with a fork to prevent puffing.
4. Bake for 10 minutes, or until set.
5. For the cream, whisk egg yolk with sugar substitute, cornstarch, and vanilla in a saucepan.
6. Heat the milk but do not boil. Gradually add to the egg mixture, stirring constantly. Return to low heat.

7. Add cocoa powder and coffee, cooking until thickened. Let the cream cool slightly.

8. Fill the oat baskets with the warm cream. Stir in some peanuts if desired.

9. Garnish each basket with a piece of dark chocolate.

Nutritional Information (Per Serving): Calories: 230 | Fat: 11g | Carbohydrates: 28g | Fiber: 3g | Sugars: 2g | Protein: 7g | Sodium: 48mg

No-Sugar-Added Berry Sorbet

Prep Time: 10 minutes | Freeze Time: 2 hours | Serves: 4

Ingredients:

- 4 cups mixed berries (fresh or frozen) (560g)
- Juice of 1 lemon (approximately 45ml)
- Optional: Sugar substitute

Instructions:

1. Blend berries, lemon juice, and sugar substitute (if using) until smooth.

2. Pour the mixture into a shallow dish and freeze for 2 hours, stirring every 30 minutes.

3. Once set, scoop and serve immediately.

Nutritional Information (Per Serving): Calories: 140 | Fat: 1g | Carbohydrates: 14g | Fiber: 6g | Sugars: 7g | Protein: 1g | Sodium: 1mg

Sugar-Free Blueberry Almond Clafoutis

Prep Time: 15 minutes | Cook Time: 25 minutes | Serves: 6

Ingredients:

- 2 cups fresh blueberries (approximately 300g)
- 4 eggs
- 1 cup almond milk (240ml)
- 3/4 cup almond flour (72g)
- 1/3 cup sugar substitute (67g)
- 1 tsp almond extract (5ml)
- Powdered sugar substitute for dusting (optional)

Instructions:

1. Preheat the oven to 375°F (190°C). Grease a pie dish and spread the blueberries evenly on the bottom.

2. In a blender, combine eggs, almond milk, almond flour, sugar substitute, and almond extract. Blend until smooth.

3. Pour the batter over the blueberries.

4. Bake for 25 minutes, or until the clafoutis is set and lightly golden.

5. Dust with powdered sugar substitute before serving, if desired.

Nutritional Information (Per Serving): Calories: 160 | Fat: 10g | Carbohydrates: 11g | Fiber: 3g | Sugars: 5g | Protein: 6g | Sodium: 41mg

Ricotta and Berry Stuffed Crepes

Prep Time: 20 minutes | Cook Time: 10 minutes | Serves: 4

Ingredients:

- 4 crepes (use low-carb crepe recipe for keto-friendly option)
- 1 cup ricotta cheese (250g)
- 1 cup mixed berries (strawberries, blueberries, raspberries) (150g)
- 2 tbsp sugar substitute (30g)
- 1 tsp vanilla extract (5ml)
- Zest of 1 lemon
- Mint leaves for garnish (optional)

Instructions:

1. In a bowl, mix ricotta with sugar substitute, vanilla extract, and lemon zest.
2. Place a crepe on a flat surface, spread a quarter of the ricotta mixture in the center, and top with a quarter of the berries.
3. Fold the crepe and repeat with the remaining crepes.
4. Garnish with mint leaves if desired.

Nutritional Information (Per Serving): Calories: 250 | Fat: 15g | Carbohydrates: 20g | Fiber: 4g | Sugars: 5g | Protein: 15g | Sodium: 185mg

Keto-Friendly Tiramisu

Prep Time: 30 minutes | Chill Time: 4 hours | Serves: 6

Ingredients:

- 1 cup heavy whipping cream (240ml)
- 1/2 cup mascarpone cheese (120g)
- 1/4 cup sugar substitute (50g)
- 1 tsp vanilla extract (5ml)
- 1 cup strong brewed coffee, cooled (240ml)
- Keto-friendly ladyfingers or sponge cake
- Unsweetened cocoa powder for dusting

Instructions:

1. In a bowl, whip the heavy cream with sugar substitute and vanilla extract until stiff peaks form.
2. Gently fold in mascarpone cheese.
3. Dip ladyfingers briefly in coffee and layer them in a serving dish.
4. Spread half of the mascarpone mixture over the ladyfingers. Repeat layers.
5. Dust with cocoa powder and refrigerate for at least 4 hours before serving.

Nutritional Information (Per Serving): Calories: 180 | Fat: 29g | Carbohydrates: 3g | Fiber: 0g | Sugars: 1g | Protein: 4g | Sodium: 32mg

Low-Carb Pumpkin Cheesecake

Prep Time: 20 minutes | Cook Time: 50 minutes | Serves: 8

Ingredients:

For the crust:

- 1 cup almond flour (96g)
- 2 tbsp butter, melted (30ml)
- 1 tbsp sugar substitute (15g)

For the filling:

- 1 can (15 oz) pumpkin puree (425g)
- 16 oz cream cheese, softened (454g)
- 1/2 cup sugar substitute (100g)
- 2 eggs
- 1 tsp vanilla extract (5ml)
- 1 tsp ground cinnamon
- 1/2 tsp ground nutmeg

Instructions:

1. Preheat the oven to 350°F (175°C).
2. Mix almond flour, melted butter, and sugar substitute for the crust. Press into the bottom of a springform pan.
3. In a bowl, beat cream cheese, pumpkin puree, sugar substitute, eggs, vanilla, cinnamon, and nutmeg until smooth.
4. Pour over the crust and smooth the top.
5. Bake for 50 minutes, or until the cheesecake is set but slightly wobbly in the center.
6. Cool and then chill in the refrigerator before serving.

Nutritional Information (Per Serving): Calories: 200 | Fat: 31g | Carbohydrates: 7g | Fiber: 2g | Sugars: 2g | Protein: 8g | Sodium: 236mg

Baked Ricotta with Lemon and Thyme

Prep Time: 10 minutes | Cook Time: 20 minutes | Serves: 4

Ingredients:

- 1 cup ricotta cheese (250g)
- Zest of 1 lemon
- 1 tbsp fresh thyme leaves
- 1 clove garlic, minced (3g)
- Salt and pepper to taste
- 1 tbsp olive oil (15ml)

Instructions:

1. Preheat the oven to 350°F (175°C).
2. In a bowl, mix ricotta with lemon zest, thyme, garlic, salt, and pepper.
3. Transfer the mixture to a baking dish, drizzle with olive oil.
4. Bake for 20 minutes or until the top is golden.

Nutritional Information (Per Serving): Calories: 155 | Fat: 12g | Carbohydrates: 2g | Fiber: 0g | Sugars: 1g | Protein: 9g | Sodium: 55mg

Nutritious Date Candies

Prep Time: 20 minutes | Chill Time: 1 hour | Serves: 12

Ingredients:

- 1 cup pitted dates (about 7 ounces) (198g)
- 1 cup walnuts (or substitute with any preferred nuts) (100g)
- 1/4 cup unsweetened shredded coconut (20g)
- 2 tbsp unsweetened cocoa powder (10g)

Instructions:

1. In a food processor, combine the walnuts and shredded coconut. Process until finely ground. If desired, you can substitute the shredded coconut with oats.
2. Add the pitted dates to the walnut-coconut mixture in the food processor. Blend until the mixture becomes uniform, thick, and slightly sticky.
3. Scoop out small portions of the mixture with a teaspoon. Roll each portion into a ball, about the size of a walnut.
4. Roll each candy ball in cocoa powder to coat.
5. Place the candies in the refrigerator for at least 1 hour to set.
6. Store the finished candies in the refrigerator. They will last up to a month.

Nutritional Information (Per Serving - 1 candy):
Calories: 85 | Fat: 5g | Carbohydrates: 11g | Fiber: 2g | Sugars: 8g | Protein: 2g | Sodium: 0mg

Egg-Free Berry Cheesecake

Prep Time: 20 minutes | Cook Time: 30-40 minutes | Serves: 8

Ingredients:

- 1 3/4 cups cottage cheese (420g)
- 1/2 cup sour cream (120g)
- 2 tbsp rice flour (16g)
- 1/4 cup honey (or a sugar substitute for a diabetic-friendly option) (60ml)
- 1 handful of mixed berries (fresh or frozen) (approximately 35g)
- Optional: extra honey or sour cream to adjust taste

Instructions:

1. Preheat the oven to 390°F (200°C). Grease a 6-inch round baking pan or line it with parchment paper.
2. In a mixing bowl, combine the cottage cheese, sour cream, rice flour, and honey. Blend with an immersion blender until smooth.
3. Pour half of the cheese mixture into the prepared pan.
4. Distribute some of the berries over this layer, lightly pressing them into the mixture.
5. Top with the remaining cheese mixture. Place the rest of the berries on top, gently pressing them in and smoothing the surface with a spatula.
6. Bake in the preheated oven for 30-40 minutes or until the cheesecake is lightly browned and slightly jiggly in the center.

7. Let the cheesecake cool completely before serving.

Nutritional Information (Per Serving): Calories: 146 | Fat: 6g | Carbohydrates: 15g | Fiber: 0.5g | Sugars: 10g | Protein: 8g | Sodium: 222mg

Low-Carb Lemon Cheesecake Bars

Prep Time: 20 minutes | Cook Time: 25 minutes | Serves: 8

Ingredients:

- 1 cup almond flour (96g)
- 1/4 cup butter, melted (60ml)
- 2 tbsp low-carb sweetener (30g)
- 8 oz cream cheese, softened (227g)
- 1/4 cup sour cream (60g)
- 2 eggs
- Zest and juice of 1 lemon
- 1 tsp vanilla extract (5ml)

Instructions:

1. Preheat the oven to 350°F (175°C). Mix almond flour, melted butter, and low-carb sweetener to form the crust. 2. Press evenly into the bottom of an 8x8 inch baking pan.

3. In a separate bowl, beat cream cheese, sour cream, eggs, lemon zest, lemon juice, and vanilla extract until smooth.

4. Pour over the crust and bake for 25 minutes.

Nutritional Information (Per Serving): Calories: 260 | Fat: 24g | Carbohydrates: 5g | Fiber: 1g | Sugars: 1g | Protein: 7g | Sodium: 177mg

Light Coffee Cheesecake without Sugar

Prep Time: 20 minutes | Cook Time: 40-45 minutes | Chill Time: 1 hour | Serves: 6

Ingredients:

- 7 ounces cottage cheese (198g)
- 5 ounces cream cheese (142g)
- 1 ripe banana
- 2 eggs
- 1/4 cup unsweetened shredded coconut (20g)
- 1 tsp instant coffee
- Optional: sugar substitute to taste

Instructions:

1. Preheat the oven to 320°F (160°C).

2. In a large bowl, mash the ripe banana with the instant coffee until smooth.

3. Add cottage cheese and cream cheese to the banana mixture. Blend until thoroughly combined.

4. Whisk in eggs one at a time, ensuring each is well incorporated before adding the next.

5. Stir in the shredded coconut.

6. Distribute the mixture evenly among the molds.

7. Bake for 40-45 minutes. Place a heatproof dish filled with hot water at the bottom of the oven to prevent the cheesecakes from drying out.

8. Turn off the oven and let the cheesecakes sit inside for an additional 30 minutes.

9. Chill the cheesecakes in the refrigerator for at least 1 hour before serving.

Nutritional Information (Per Serving): Calories: 183 | Fat: 13g | Carbohydrates: 6g | Fiber: 1g | Sugars: 3g | Protein: 9g | Sodium: 250mg

Oat Baskets with Cottage Cheese and Berries

Prep Time: 25 minutes | Cook Time: 25 minutes | Serves: 6

Ingredients:

- 1/3 cup rolled oats (30g)
- 2 tbsp almond flour (or ground nuts) (14g)
- 1 egg white
- 1 cup cottage cheese (226g)
- Sugar substitute to taste
- 1/2 tsp agar-agar powder or pectin
- A handful of mixed berries (approximately 35g)
- 1 tsp honey (5ml)
- A pinch of salt
- Optional: oil for greasing tartlet molds

Instructions:

1. Preheat the oven to 390°F (200°C).
2. Mix rolled oats, almond flour, egg white, honey, and a pinch of salt in a bowl to form a pliable dough. Add more oats or flour if the mixture is too sticky.
3. Press the dough into the molds, making small baskets. Bake for 10 minutes.
4. Blend cottage cheese with sugar substitute and egg yolk until smooth.

5. Fill the baked oat baskets with the cottage cheese mixture. Bake for another 10-15 minutes at 375°F (190°C).
6. Let the baskets cool on a wire rack.
Meanwhile, mix agar-agar with 1/3 cup water. Bring to a boil, then let it cool slightly until it begins to thicken.
7. Top the baskets with berries and brush them with the agar-agar gel.
8. Serve the oat baskets once the agar-agar has set.

Nutritional Information (Per Serving): Calories: 112 | Fat: 3g | Carbohydrates: 11g | Fiber: 2g | Sugars: 4g | Protein: 10g | Sodium: 270mg

Cottage Cheese Dessert with Blueberries

Prep Time: 15 minutes | Serves: 2

Ingredients:

- 1 cup cottage cheese (about 8 ounces) (227g)
- 2 tbsp condensed milk (or sugar substitute for a diabetic-friendly option) (30ml)
- 1/4 cup unsweetened cornflakes (20g)
- 2 tbsp drinkable yogurt (strawberry flavored or any preferred flavor) (30ml)
- 1 tsp sugar-free vanilla extract (5ml)
- 1/2 cup blueberries (72g)

Instructions:

1. Divide the cottage cheese into two bowls. To one bowl, add condensed milk, half of the blueberries (about 1/4 cup), and half the sugar-free. In the other bowl, add yogurt and the remaining sugar-free vanilla.
2. Blend or mash the contents of each bowl until smooth.
3. Prepare two serving dishes or jars. Layer the bottom with the cottage cheese mixture containing blueberries.
4. Sprinkle a layer of unsweetened cornflakes over the first layer of cottage cheese.
5. Add a layer of the white cottage cheese mixture on top of the unsweetened cornflakes.
6. Randomly place the remaining blueberries on top.
7. Add another layer of the blueberry cottage cheese mixture, followed by a final layer of unsweetened cornflakes.
8. Top with the remaining white cottage cheese mixture. Garnish with a few blueberries and mint leaves, if desired.

Nutritional Information (Per Serving): Calories: 200 | Fat: 14g | Protein: 14g | Carbohydrates: 28g | Sugars: 2g | Fiber: 12g | Sodium: 320mg

Baked Apples with Cottage Cheese

Prep Time: 15 minutes | Cook Time: 30 minutes | Serves: 6

Ingredients:

- 6 apples (any color or variety, firm but not too soft)
- ⅔ cup cottage cheese (150g) (Choose a low-carb, unsweetened variety)
- 1 egg yolk
- 2 tbsp powdered sugar substitute with zero or low carbs (16g)
- 1 tsp sugar-free vanilla extract
- 1 tsp cornstarch (3.4g) (Optional, but use a low-carb alternative if desired)
- Optional: Raisins (ensure they are low-carb and sugar-free)

Instructions:

1. Preheat the oven to 375°F (190°C).
2. Wash the apples. Cut off the tops to create 'lids' and carefully scoop out the cores with a teaspoon, making sure not to pierce through the bottom or sides.
3. In a blender, combine cottage cheese, powdered sugar substitute, cornstarch (if used), vanilla extract, and egg yolk. Blend until smooth. Optionally, you can stir in some raisins, but ensure they are low-carb and sugar-free.
4. Place the apples in a buttered baking dish. Fill each apple with the low-carb cottage cheese mixture.
5. Bake in the preheated oven for about 30 minutes or until the apples are soft (test with a knife).
6. Serve warm, optionally sprinkled with more powdered sugar substitute for sweetness, keeping the total carbohydrates and sugars within your desired limits.

Nutritional Information (Per Serving): Calories: 130 | Fat: 3g | Protein: 5g | Carbohydrates: 26g | Sugars: 15g | Fiber: 4g | Sodium: 75mg.

Red Fish Tartlets

Prep time: 30 minutes | Cook Time: 0 minutes (assembly only) | Serves: 6

Ingredients:

- 6 premade tartlet shells
- 3.5 ounces red fish (like salmon), thinly sliced (100g)
- 2 small cucumbers
- 3.5 ounces low-fat cottage cheese (100g)
- 2 sprigs of dill, finely chopped (or a mix of dry herbs)
- Optional: Microgreens, sesame seeds, fresh or dry basil for garnish

Instructions:

1. Combine the chopped dill with cottage cheese.
2. Evenly distribute the cottage cheese mixture into the tartlet shells.
3. Thinly slice the cucumbers. Roll cucumber slices into tubes and place 2-3 in each tartlet.
4. Cut the red fish into uniform, thin pieces without skin. Roll and place them in each tartlet.
5. Garnish the tartlets with microgreens, sesame seeds, basil, or any preferred greens.
6. Store the prepared tartlets for up to 24 hours in the refrigerator.

Nutritional Information (Per Serving): Calories: 400 | Fat: 6g | Protein: 8g | Carbohydrates: 9g | Sugars: 2g | Fiber: 1g | Sodium: 170mg.

Mediterranean Tuna and White Bean

Prep Time: 15 minutes | Cook Time: 0 minutes | Serves: 4

Ingredients:

- 2 cans of tuna in water, drained (approximately 10 oz total or 280g)
- 1 can white beans, drained and rinsed (approximately 15 oz or 425g)
- 1 cup cherry tomatoes, halved (150g)
- 1 cucumber, diced (200g)
- 1/2 red onion, thinly sliced (approximately 60g)
- 1/4 cup chopped fresh parsley
- 3 tbsp olive oil (45ml)
- Juice of 1 lemon (approximately 45ml)
- Salt and pepper to taste

Instructions:

1. In a large bowl, combine tuna, white beans, cherry tomatoes, cucumber, red onion, and parsley.
2. Whisk together olive oil, lemon juice, salt, and pepper.

3. Pour the dressing over the salad and toss gently to combine.

Nutritional Information (Per Serving): Calories: 400 | Fat: 14g | Protein: 31g | Carbohydrates: 25g | Sugars: 3g | Fiber: 6g | Sodium: 550mg.

Grilled Salmon with Avocado Salsa

Prep Time: 15 minutes | Cook Time: 10 minutes | Serves: 4

Ingredients:

- 4 salmon fillets, about 6 ounces each (170g each)
- 2 ripe avocados, diced (450g total)
- 1/2 red onion, finely chopped (60g)
- 1 tomato, diced (150g)
- Juice of 1 lime (30ml)
- 2 tbsp olive oil (30ml)
- Salt and pepper to taste
- Fresh cilantro, chopped for garnish

Instructions:

1. Preheat grill to medium heat.
2. Brush salmon with olive oil, season with salt and pepper.
3. Grill salmon for about 5 minutes on each side, or until cooked to your liking.
4. In a bowl, mix avocado, red onion, tomato, lime juice, and salt.
5. Serve grilled salmon topped with avocado salsa and garnished with cilantro.

Nutritional Information (Per Serving): Calories: 450 | Fat: 26g | Protein: 30g | Carbohydrates: 16g | Sugars: 2g | Fiber: 9g | Sodium: 280mg.

Grilled Tuna Steaks with Olive Tapenade

Prep Time: 15 minutes | Cook Time: 10 minutes | Serves: 4

Ingredients:

- 4 tuna steaks, about 6 ounces each (170g each)
- 1 cup mixed olives, pitted (approximately 150g)
- 2 tbsp capers
- 2 cloves garlic
- 1/4 cup olive oil (60ml)
- Juice of 1 lemon (45ml)
- Salt and pepper to taste

Instructions:

1. Preheat grill to medium-high heat.
2. Season tuna steaks with salt and pepper.
3. Grill tuna for about 4-5 minutes on each side, or to desired doneness.
4. For the tapenade, blend olives, capers, garlic, olive oil, and lemon juice in a food processor until smooth.
5. Serve grilled tuna with a dollop of olive tapenade on top.

Nutritional Information (Per Serving): Calories: 450 | Fat: 25g | Protein: 35g | Carbohydrates: 5g | Sugars: 1g | Fiber: 2g | Sodium: 800mg.

5. Pour in the broth and coconut milk, bring to a simmer.

6. Add fish and shrimp to the pot. Cook for about 5 minutes, until the seafood is cooked through.

7. Stir in the remaining lime juice and cilantro. Adjust seasoning with salt.

8. Let the stew rest for 5 minutes before serving.

9. Serve garnished with lime slices and additional cilantro if desired.

Nutritional Information (Per Serving): Calories: 420 | Fat: 22g | Protein: 32g | Carbohydrates: 17g | Sugars: 5g | Fiber: 3g | Sodium: 800mg.

Fish Stew with Shrimp and Coconut Milk

Prep Time: 30 minutes | Cook Time: 20 minutes | Serves: 4

Ingredients:

- 1 3/4 cups fish or vegetable broth (420ml)
- 14 ounces white fish fillet (like cod or tilapia), cut into 1-inch cubes (397g)
- 9 ounces shrimp, peeled and deveined (255g)
- 1 cup coconut milk (240ml)
- 1 large tomato, diced (or 1 cup canned diced tomatoes) (180g)
- 1 large bell pepper, thinly sliced (150g)
- 1 onion, finely chopped (150g)
- Juice of 1 lime (approximately 45ml)
- 1 tbsp chopped cilantro (cilantro)
- 2 cloves garlic, minced
- 1 small chili pepper, finely chopped (adjust to taste)
- 3 tbsp olive oil (45ml)
- Salt to taste

Instructions:

1. Marinate fish and shrimp in half the lime juice, 1 tablespoon olive oil, and a pinch of salt. Cover and refrigerate.

2. In a blender, combine the tomatoes, chili pepper, half the onion, half the bell pepper, and garlic. Blend until coarse, not completely smooth.

3. In a pot, sauté the remaining onion and bell pepper in 2 tablespoons of olive oil for 5 minutes.

4. Add the blended mixture to the pot and cook for another 5 minutes.

Classic Marinated Fish Recipe

Prep Time: 35 minutes | Cook Time: 25 minutes | Serves: 4

Ingredients:

- 1.1 pounds pollock or a similar white fish, cut into small pieces (500g)
- 1 large onion, sliced
- 2 medium carrots, sliced
- 5 tbsp vegetable oil (75ml)
- 3 tbsp tomato paste (45ml)
- 3 tbsp all-purpose flour (23g)
- 1 bay leaf
- 1 tsp salt
- 1 tbsp vinegar (9% acidity) (15ml)
- 10 whole black peppercorns
- 1 1/4 cups water (300ml)

Instructions:

1. Sauté onions and carrots for 10-13 minutes until the onions are golden and the carrots are softened.

2. Add tomato paste, bay leaf, whole black peppercorns, salt and water to the skillet. Mix well.

3. Simmer the marinade for about 15 minutes on low heat. Then add vinegar and bring to a boil. Remove from heat. The marinade should be a little tangy and rich in flavor.

4. Fish fillets cut into small pieces. Lightly salt and coat each piece in flour.

5. In a separate pan, heat the remaining oil. Fry the fish for 1-1.5 min on each side until golden brown.

6. In a dish, layer half of the vegetable marinade, then the fish, and top with the remaining marinade.

7. Refrigerate the marinated fish for at least 1 hour, preferably longer, to allow the flavors to meld. Garnish with parsley or green onions.

Nutritional Information (Per Serving): Calories: 350 | Fat: 23g | Protein: 34g | Carbohydrates: 20g | Sugars: 5g | Fiber: 3g | Sodium: 695mg.

Lemon-Garlic Shrimp with Zucchini Noodles

Prep Time: 20 minutes | Cook Time: 10 minutes | Serves: 4

Ingredients:

- 1 pound shrimp, peeled and deveined (450g)
- 4 medium zucchinis, spiralized into noodles (1200g)
- 3 cloves garlic, minced
- Juice and zest of 1 lemon (45ml juice)
- 2 tbsp olive oil (30ml)
- Salt and pepper to taste
- Fresh parsley

Instructions:

1. In a large pan, heat 1 tablespoon olive oil over medium heat.

2. Sauté garlic until fragrant, then add shrimp, cooking until pink and opaque.

3. Remove shrimp and add remaining olive oil.

4. Cook zucchini noodles in the same pan for about 2 minutes.

5. Return shrimp to the pan, add lemon juice and zest, and season with salt and pepper.

6. Garnish with parsley before serving.

Nutritional Information (Per Serving): Calories: 410 | Fat: 9g | Protein: 28g | Carbohydrates: 14g | Sugars: 7g | Fiber: 4g | Sodium: 290mg.

Chopped Red Fish Patties

Prep Time: 20 minutes | Cook Time: 5 minutes | Serves: 4

Ingredients:

- 1.1 pounds red fish fillet (like salmon), cut into small cubes (500g)
- 1 large egg
- 1 1/2 tbsp all-purpose flour (11g)
- 1 ounce green onions, finely chopped (28g)
- 1 1/2 tbsp sour cream (22ml)
- 1 tbsp fresh dill, chopped
- 1 tbsp lemon juice (15ml)
- 1/2 tsp dried Italian herbs or rosemary
- 1 1/2 tbsp vegetable oil (22ml)
- A pinch of mixed peppercorns, crushed
- 1/4 tsp salt, or to taste
- Optional: 1/2 clove garlic, minced

Instructions:

1. In a bowl, mix together the cubed red fish and egg.
2. Add green onions, dill, garlic, Italian herbs, lemon juice, and sour cream. Mix well. Season with salt and crushed peppercorns.
3. Gently stir in the flour until well combined.
4. Spoon the fish mixture into the skillet heat, forming round patties.
5. Cook each patty for about 1.5-2 minutes per side or until golden brown and cooked through.
6. Serve the patties with a side of white sauce, lemon slices, and your choice of vegetable garnish or on a sandwich.

Nutritional Information (Per Serving): Calories: 420 | Fat: 11g | Protein: 22g | Carbohydrates: 6g | Sugars: 1g | Fiber: 1g | Sodium: 300mg.

Couscous with Fish and Tomatoes

Prep Time: 20 minutes | Cook Time: 25 minutes | Serves: 4

Ingredients:

- 8.8 ounces white fish fillet (like cod, haddock, or tilapia), cut into pieces (250g)
- 1/2 cup canned diced tomatoes (120g)
- 1/6 of a large onion, finely chopped (25g)
- 1/6 of a large red bell pepper, finely chopped (25g)
- 1/6 bunch of parsley
- 3/4 cup couscous (120g)
- 1 tbsp vegetable oil (15ml)
- Salt and spices to taste
- 1/2 cup water (120ml)

Instructions:

1. 1. Preheat your oven to 350°F (180°C).
2. Sauté the onion and bell pepper for about 3-4 minutes until softened.
3. Cut the fish into small pieces. Add the fish to the skillet and cook for about 5 minutes.
4. Stir in the diced tomatoes. Season with salt and your choice of spices (like dry garlic, Provencal or Italian herbs).
5. Rinse the can with 1/3 cup hot water and add to the skillet.
6. Cook everything for 15 min on low heat, covered.
7. Add the couscous to the skillet, stir, cover, and turn off the heat. Let it sit for about 5 minutes.
8. Garnish with chopped parsley.

Nutritional Information (Per Serving): Calories: 320 | Fat: 5g | Protein: 22g | Carbohydrates: 30g | Sugars: 2g | Fiber: 4g | Sodium: 300mg.

White Fish in Creamy Garlic Sauce

Prep Time: 15 minutes | Cook Time: 40 minutes | Serves: 4

Ingredients:

- 1.3 pounds white fish fillets (like cod, haddock, pollock), cut into pieces (590g)
- 1 1/4 cups sour cream (10-15% fat) (300g)
- 2 egg yolks
- 2 cloves garlic, minced
- Spices (such as dill, parsley, black pepper)
- 1/2 tsp salt, or to taste
- Optional: fresh herbs for garnishing

Instructions:

1. Preheat oven to 350°F (180°C).
2. In a bowl, whisk together sour cream, egg yolks, garlic, salt, and spices until smooth.
3. Place fish pieces in a baking dish.
4. Pour the sour cream mixture over the fish, ensuring it's evenly coated.
5. Bake in the preheated oven for 35-40 minutes, or until the fish is cooked through and the top is slightly golden.
6. Serve with a garnish of fresh herbs and your choice of side, such as fresh or cooked vegetables, rice, or mashed potatoes.

Nutritional Information (Per Serving): Calories: 370 | Fat: 19g | Protein: 31g | Carbohydrates: 6g | Sugars: 2g | Fiber: 0g | Sodium: 400mg.

Salad with Marinated Mussels

Prep Time: 20 minutes | Cook Time: 10 minutes | Serves: 2

Ingredients:

- 7 ounces marinated mussels (198g)
- 1/2 small red onion, thinly sliced (50g)
- 1 large tomato, diced (180g)
- A handful of green olives, halved (pitted) (30g)
- 2 hard-boiled eggs, sliced
- 5 sprigs of parsley, finely chopped
- 2 tbsp sour cream (30ml)
- Salt to taste
- Optional: fresh ground pepper, lemon juice

Instructions:

1. Thinly slice the red onion and dice the tomato. If desired, let the tomato drain in a sieve to remove excess liquid.
2. Drain the marinated mussels. If using plain cooked mussels, consider adding a squeeze of lemon juice and some extra spices.
3. In a salad bowl, gently mix the mussels, onion, tomato, olives, and egg slices.
4. Dress the salad with sour cream and toss lightly. Season with salt and optional pepper.
5. Garnish with chopped parsley.

Nutritional Information (Per Serving): Calories: 250 | Fat: 20g | Protein: 19g | Carbohydrates: 22g | Sugars: 6g | Fiber: 4g | Sodium: 900mg.

Butterfish Steak with Vegetables

Prep Time: 20 minutes | Cook Time: 15 minutes | Serves: 2

Ingredients:

- 10.5 ounces (about 2/3 pound) butterfish, or a similar white fish (297g)
- 1 tomato, sliced (150g)
- 1 large bell pepper, sliced into strips (150g)
- 1/4 cup green olives, sliced (37.5g)
- 2 tbsp fresh cilantro, chopped
- 1 tbsp olive oil (15ml)
- 1/2 tsp dried oregano
- Pinch of black pepper
- 1/2 tsp salt, or to taste
- Optional: 1 clove garlic, minced.

Instructions:

1. Preheat a skillet over medium heat and brush with olive oil.
2. Place the fish steak in the skillet, cook until golden on one side, then flip. Season the fish with salt and pepper.
3. Add the bell pepper, tomato, and olives to the skillet. Cover and cook for a few minutes until the vegetables are tender but still slightly crisp.
4. Sprinkle oregano and cilantro over the vegetables and fish. Add garlic or other spices if desired. Cook covered for another minute.
5. Serve the fish steak with the sautéed vegetables and a lemon slice on the side.

Nutritional Information (Per Serving): Calories: 420 | Fat: 13g | Protein: 26g | Carbohydrates: 17g | Sugars: 5g | Fiber: 4g | Sodium: 800mg.

Squid Salad with Mushrooms

Prep Time: 20 minutes | Cook Time: 10 minutes | Serves: 2

Ingredients:

- 5 oz squid, cleaned and sliced into rings (142g)
- 3 oz mushrooms, thinly sliced (85g)
- 2.5 oz mozzarella cheese, cut into long strips (71g)
- 1.5 oz black olives, pitted and sliced (43g)
- Vegetable oil, as needed
- Optional: a handful of nuts, crushed (e.g., walnuts)
- Lettuce leaves, as needed for the salad base

Instructions:

1. Boil the squid in water with black peppercorns, a slice of lemon, and a sprig of dill for 2 minutes, then plunge into cold water. Peel off the skin and slice into rings.
2. Sauté the mushrooms in a bit of vegetable oil until tender.
3. In a salad bowl, combine the squid rings, mushrooms, mozzarella strips, and sliced olives.
4. Tear lettuce leaves and add them to the bowl. Optionally, add crushed nuts for an extra crunch.
5. Toss the salad gently. You can either dress it with a classic vinaigrette or leave it undressed, as the mushrooms and olives provide enough moisture and flavor.

Nutritional Information (Per Serving): Calories: 230 | Fat: 17g | Protein: 18g | Carbohydrates: 11g | Sugars: 3g | Fiber: 4g | Sodium: 650mg.

Cajun Shrimp and Cauliflower Grits

Prep Time: 15 minutes | Cook Time: 20 minutes | Serves: 4

Ingredients:

- 1 pound shrimp, peeled and deveined (450g)
- 2 tbsp Cajun seasoning
- 1 head cauliflower, grated (500g)
- 1 cup chicken broth (240ml)
- 1/2 cup grated Parmesan cheese (50g)
- 2 tbsp olive oil (30ml)
- Salt and pepper to taste
- Green onions, sliced for garnish

Instructions:

1. Toss shrimp with Cajun seasoning.
2. In a skillet, heat 1 tablespoon olive oil and cook shrimp until pink, about 3-4 min per side. Set aside.
3. In the same skillet, add grated cauliflower, chicken broth, salt, and pepper. Cook until tender. Stir in Parmesan cheese until creamy.
4. Serve shrimp over cauliflower grits, garnished with green onions.

Nutritional Information (Per Serving): Calories: 420 | Fat: 12g | Protein: 30g | Carbohydrates: 12g | Sugars: 3g | Fiber: 4g | Sodium: 950mg.

Arugula Salad with Cherry Tomatoes and Mussels

Prep Time: 20 minutes | Cook Time: 10 minutes | Serves: 2

Ingredients:

- 7 ounces mussels, cleaned and cooked (198g)
- 1 cup cherry tomatoes, halved (150g)
- 2 cups arugula (40g)
- 1 small red bell pepper, seeded and chopped (approximately 75g)
- 1/2 small red onion, thinly sliced (50g)
- 2 cloves garlic, minced
- 2 tbsp pesto sauce
- 1 tbsp balsamic vinegar
- 2 tbsp olive oil
- Mixed herbs (like Provencal herbs) and salt to taste
- Optional: 1 tbsp finely chopped nuts (any variety)

Instructions:

1. Lightly sauté the bell pepper in a bit of olive oil until slightly softened, about 3 minutes.
2. Sauté garlic in olive oil with half a teaspoon of mixed herbs for a minute, then add the mussels and cook for another 2 minutes. Let cool slightly.
3. For the dressing, mix pesto with balsamic vinegar, olive oil, and optional chopped nuts. Shake well to combine.
4. In a salad bowl, combine arugula, bell pepper, cherry tomatoes, and mussels.
5. Drizzle with the prepared dressing and toss gently. Garnish with red onion rings.

Nutritional Information (Per Serving): Calories: 350 |Fat: 20g | Protein: 12g | Carbohydrates: 15g | Sugars: 6g | Fiber: 3g | Sodium: 450mg.

Zucchini Rolls with Fish and Shrimp

Prep Time: 35 minutes | Cook Time: 40 minutes | Serves: 4

Ingredients:

- 12 ounces fish fillet (such as salmon or white fish), thinly sliced (340g)
- 9 medium shrimp, deveined (tail on for decoration)
- 2 medium zucchinis, sliced into thin strips (500g)
- 2 cloves garlic, minced
- Juice of 1/2 lemon (15ml)
- 3 tbsp vegetable oil
- Spices (such as dill, parsley, black pepper) to taste
- Salt to taste

Instructions:

1. Slice the zucchinis into very thin strips.
2. Slice the fish fillet into thin strips, approximately the same size as the zucchini strips.
3. In a bowl, mix the fish slices with lemon juice, minced garlic, spices, salt. Marinate for 15-20 min.
4. Clean the shrimp, add to the fish marinade and let sit for an additional 5-7 minutes.
5. To assemble the rolls, place a slice of marinated fish on a zucchini strip, add a shrimp, and roll tightly. Secure each roll with a toothpick.
6. Brush the rolls with vegetable oil and bake in a preheated oven at 350°F (180°C) until cooked through, about 40 minutes.
7. Serve the rolls with a fresh vegetable salad or as a standalone dish.

Nutritional Information (Per Serving): Calories: 320 | Fat: 11g | Protein: 24g | Carbohydrates: 12g | Sugars: 5g | Fiber: 3g | Sodium: 370mg.

Fried Mussels

Prep Time: 15 minutes | Cook Time: 10 minutes | Serves: 4

Ingredients:

- 1.1 pounds mussels, cleaned (500g)
- 2 large onions, thinly sliced into half-rings (300g)
- 2 tbsp vegetable oil
- Salt and black pepper
- Fresh herbs (like parsley or green onions), chopped for garnish

Instructions:

1. Clean and thinly slice the onions.
2. Heat the vegetable oil in a large skillet over medium-high heat.
3. Add the onions to the skillet and sauté until they are golden brown and soft.
4. Increase the heat and add the mussels to the skillet. Cook for a maximum of 5 minutes, stirring occasionally.
5. Once the mussels are cooked, season with salt and pepper to taste.
6. Garnish with chopped fresh parsley or green onions. Serve hot with fresh tomatoes and soft white bread.

Nutritional Information (Per Serving): Calories: 220 | Fat: 8g | Protein: 21g | Carbohydrates: 12g | Sugars: 4g | Fiber: 2g | Sodium: 420mg.

Rice with Squid and Egg

Prep Time: 15 minutes | Cook Time: 20 minutes | Serves: 2

Ingredients:

- 1 cup long-grain rice
- 1 small squid, boiled and sliced into rings
- 1/4 of a medium red onion, finely chopped
- 1/4 of a spicy pepper, finely chopped (adjust to taste)
- 4 sprigs of dill, finely chopped (parsley can be a substitute)
- 1.5 tsp vegetable oil
- Salt to taste
- 1 egg
- 1/2 clove of garlic, minced
- 1.5 tsp soy sauce

Instructions:

1. Cook rice in salted water.
2. In a small bowl, beat the egg with a pinch of salt.
3. Heat half of the vegetable oil in a skillet and scramble the egg. Remove and set aside.
4. In another skillet, heat the remaining oil. Add onion, garlic, and spicy pepper. Sauté for a few minutes, stirring frequently.
5. Add cooked rice, squid, dill, and scrambled egg to the skillet. Pour in the soy sauce. Cook, stirring, for a few minutes.
6. Taste and adjust seasoning, adding salt if needed.
7. Serve hot, optionally garnished with toasted sesame seeds.

Nutritional Information (Per Serving): Calories: 350 | Fat: 5g | Protein: 16g | Carbohydrates: 63g | Sugars: 1g | Fiber: 1g | Sodium: 550mg.

Creamy Fish and Broccoli Quiche Baked in the Oven

Prep time: 1 hour | Cook Time: 55 minutes | Serves: 6

Ingredients:

For the Crust:

- 1 1/3 cups all-purpose flour (167g)
- 6 tbsp unsalted butter, chilled and cubed
- 1 large egg
- Pinch of salt

For the Filling:

- 11 ounces fish fillet (like cod or salmon), cut into small pieces (312g)

- 1 1/4 cups broccoli florets (about 94g)
- 2/3 cup light cream (about 10% fat) (160ml)
- 4 large eggs
- Salt, black pepper, and ground nutmeg to taste
- 1 tbsp chopped parsley
- Olive oil or butter for greasing

Instructions:

1. For the crust, sift flour into a bowl. Rub in chilled butter until mixture resembles fine breadcrumbs.
2. Beat 1 egg with a fork and mix into the flour until a dough forms. Wrap in plastic and chill for 30 minutes.
3. Preheat the oven to 390°F (200°C).
4. Roll out the dough on a floured surface to fit a 9-inch tart pan. Place dough in the pan, press into the edges, and trim excess. Prick the base with a fork.
5. Bake the crust for 15-20 min until lightly golden.
6. Blanch broccoli in boiling salted water for 3-4 minutes, then rinse with cold water and drain.
7. Whisk together 4 eggs, cream, salt, pepper, nutmeg, and parsley for the filling.
8. Arrange fish pieces and broccoli on the pre-baked crust.
9. Pour the egg mixture over the fish and broccoli.
10. Bake for 30-35 minutes at 355°F (180°C) until the filling is set and slightly golden.
11. Let cool slightly, cut into slices, and serve.

Nutritional Information (Per Serving): Calories: 450 | 360 | Fat: 20g | Protein: 18g | Carbohydrates: 29g | Sugars: 1g | Fiber: 2g | Sodium: 220mg.

Fish in Parchment with Cherry Tomatoes

Prep Time: 15 minutes | Cook Time: 25 minutes | Serves: 4

Ingredients:

- 12.3 ounces of fresh white fish fillet (like cod, haddock, or perch) (349g)
- 12 cherry tomatoes, halved
- 1 tbsp olive oil
- 3 ounces mozzarella cheese, sliced (85g)
- 1 handful of fresh herbs (parsley and basil), chopped
- 1 small garlic clove
- Salt and mixed spices for fish to taste
- Optional: mixed nuts, finely chopped

Instructions:

1. Preheat the oven to 350°F (180°C).
2. Brush parchment paper with olive oil and add fish. Season the fish with salt and mixed spices.
3. In a blender, combine herbs, garlic, 2 teaspoons of olive oil, and optional nuts to make a paste. Spread this paste over the fish.
4. Top the fish with cherry tomato halves and mozzarella slices.
5. Fold the parchment paper into tight envelopes, sealing the edges to keep the juices in.
6. Bake for about 25 minutes until the fish is cooked through.

Nutritional Information (Per Serving): Calories: 300 |220 | Fat: 12g | Protein: 23g | Carbohydrates: 6g | Sugars: 2g | Fiber: 1g | Sodium: 280mg.

Blue Pancakes with Fish Filling

Prep Time: 30 minutes | Cook Time: 20 minutes | Serves: 4

Ingredients:

For Pancakes:

- 3 cups unsweetened almond milk (720ml)
- 4 large eggs
- 2 cups red cabbage, finely chopped (200g)
- 1 1/4 cups almond flour (156g)
- 1 1/4 cups coconut flour (160g)
- 1 tbsp vegetable oil (15ml)
- A pinch of salt

For Filling:

- 6 ounces smoked salmon, chopped (170g)
- 1/2 cup cottage cheese (113g)
- Fresh herbs (like dill or parsley), chopped

Instructions:

1. Blend the red cabbage to extract about 1/2 cup juice. Add more cabbage if needed.
2. Whisk together almond milk, eggs, almond flour, coconut flour, cabbage juice, vegetable oil, and salt until smooth for the pancake batter.
3. Cook low-carb pancakes in a non-stick skillet over medium heat, using a little oil if desired.
4. For the filling, mix smoked salmon, cottage cheese, and chopped herbs. Place 2-3 tablespoons of filling on each pancake, fold envelope-style.
5. Serve immediately with a dollop of sour cream and extra herbs, if desired.

Nutritional Information (Per Serving): Calories: 340 | Fat: 17g | Protein: 22g | Carbohydrates: 25g | Sugars: 5g | Fiber: 13g | Sodium: 480mg.

Creamy Mussel Soup

Prep Time: 20 minutes | Cook Time: 30 minutes | Serves: 4

Ingredients:

- 1 pound frozen mussels, thawed (450g)
- 1/4 cup dry white wine (60ml)
- 3 slices bacon, chopped
- 1 small onion, thinly sliced (70g)
- 1/3 cup rice (65g)
- 1 leek, white and light green parts only (100g)
- 3/4 cup heavy cream (180ml)
- Black pepper to taste
- 1 carrot, thinly sliced (60g)
- 2 cloves garlic, minced (6g)
- 2 tbsp olive oil (30ml)
- 1 tbsp butter (14g)
- 2 bay leaves
- 1 small chili pepper, sliced
- Salt to taste
- Parsley, chopped for garnish

Instructions:

1. Blanch mussels in boiling water for 4 minutes, drain and set aside.
2. Sauté bacon, onion, carrot, leek, and garlic in a mix of olive oil and butter until soft.
3. Add rice and cook for another 2 minutes.
4. Transfer the sautéed mixture to a pot, add 6 cups of hot water, and bring to a gentle simmer.
5. Add mussels, wine, salt, pepper, and bay leaves. Cook for 5 minutes.
6. Stir in heavy cream and adjust seasoning. Heat through without boiling.

7. Serve garnished with carrot 'stars', fresh parsley, and optional chili pepper slices.

Nutritional Information (Per Serving): Calories: 380 | Fat: 26g | Protein: 10g | Carbohydrates: 23g | Sugars: 3g | Fiber: 1g | Sodium: 430mg.

Glass Noodle Seafood Stir-Fry

Prep Time: 20 minutes | Cook Time: 10 minutes | Serves: 4

Ingredients:

- 3.5 oz glass noodles (100g)
- 5.3 oz shrimp, cleaned (150g)
- 5.3 oz mussels, cleaned (150g)
- 1 small red onion, thinly sliced (70g)
- A small bunch of green onions, sliced diagonally
- 1 large bell pepper, julienned (150g)
- 1 clove garlic, minced (3g)
- 1/2 tsp sugar
- 1/2 tsp ground coriander
- 1/2 tsp ground ginger
- 1/2 tsp paprika
- 1/2 tsp vegetable oil (2.5ml)
- 2 tbsp soy sauce (30ml)
- 2 tbsp balsamic vinegar (30ml)
- A pinch of sesame seeds
- A pinch of cumin
- A pinch of black pepper
- A pinch of salt

Instructions:

1. Soak glass noodles in warm water as per package instructions until they are soft.
2. Slice red onion and bell pepper. Chop green onions.

3. Thaw shrimp and mussels, if frozen. Clean and prepare them.

4. Sauté red onion and bell pepper in a skillet with vegetable oil until slightly softened.

5. Add seafood and garlic, stir-fry for 2-3 minutes.

6. Combine soy sauce, balsamic vinegar, ground coriander, ginger, paprika, sugar, black pepper, and salt in a bowl.

7. Add this mixture to the skillet, stir well.

8. Drain the glass noodles and add to the skillet. Toss everything together and heat through.

9. Garnish with green onions, sesame seeds, and cumin.

Nutritional Information (Per Serving): Calories: 320 | Fat: 2g | Protein: 21g | Carbohydrates: 33g | Sugars: 4g | Fiber: 3g | Sodium: 740mg.

Classic Seafood Paella

Prep Time: 20 minutes | Cook Time: 30 minutes | Serves: 4

Ingredients:

- 1 cup wild rice
- 2.5 cups water (600ml)
- 1 small shallot, finely chopped
- 1 lime, cut into wedges
- 1 medium tomato, diced (150g)
- 1 cup green beans, trimmed and halved (100g)
- 8.8 ounces white fish fillet, like walleye (cut into pieces) (250g)
- 1 medium bell pepper, julienned (150g)
- 8.8 ounces shrimp, peeled and deveined (250g)
- 3.5 ounces mussels (100g)
- 3.5 ounces calamari, cleaned and sliced (100g)
- 3.5 ounces octopus, cleaned and chopped (100g)
- 1/2 teaspoon saffron threads
- 1 sprig rosemary
- 3 tbsp olive oil, divided
- 1/2 tsp salt
- 2 pinches black pepper

Instructions:

1. Soak saffron in 50 ml of warm water.

2. Sauté shallots in half the olive oil with rosemary until golden. Remove rosemary.

3. Add bell pepper and tomato to the pan, cook for a few minutes.

4. Add green beans, cook for 1-2 minutes.

5. Rinse rice under cold water, add to the pan with vegetables. Cook for 2-3 minutes.

6. Add water, saffron infusion, salt, and black pepper. Cook rice on low heat for 15-18 minutes.

7. Sauté fish, calamari, octopus, and mussels in remaining olive oil. Season with salt.

8. When rice is nearly cooked, add seafood on top. Cover and cook for 3-4 minutes.

9. Add shrimp towards the end of cooking.

10. Let the paella rest for 15-20 minutes before serving. Garnish with lime wedges.

Nutritional Information (Per Serving): Calories: 450 | Fat: 11g | Protein: 47g | Carbohydrates: 15g | Sugars: 5g | Fiber: 4g | Sodium: 589mg

CHAPTER 7: BONUSES

Meal Plans and Shopping Templates: Ready-to-use templates to simplify meal planning.

To support your healthy and delicious low-carb journey, we've crafted a 30-day grocery shopping template. This template is designed to make meal preparation seamless and stress-free. It focuses on fresh, whole foods, minimizing processed items and added sugars. Adjust the quantities as needed to fit your household and dietary preferences.

Remember to always check labels for hidden sugars and carbs, especially in sauces and dressings. Opt for fresh, whole foods as much as possible, and enjoy the process of cooking and eating healthily. Happy cooking and savoring every bite!

Grocery Shopping List for 7-Day Meal Plan

Proteins

Buckwheat
Chicken breast (for soup)
Cottage cheese
Salmon fillets (for grilling and tartlets)
Tuna (for salad)
Beef (for goulash soup and medallions)
Egg (for various dishes)
Shrimp (for stew and salad)
Assorted seafood (for paella and marinated fish)
Pork (for cream sauce dish)

Vegetables & Herbs

Cauliflower (for rice bowl)
Onions (red, shallots)
Sweet peppers (various colors)
Zucchini (for pancakes and noodles)
Cherry tomatoes (for salads)
Avocado (for salsa and trifle)
Lemon (for tart and dressing)
Mushrooms (for soups and pork dish)
Bell peppers (for pork dish)
Garlic
Fresh herbs (parsley, rosemary, dill)
Fennel (if required)
Cucumber
Asparagus

Dairy and Dairy Alternatives

Greek yogurt (if needed)
Mozzarella cheese (for salad and stuffed chicken)
Heavy cream (for soups and sauces)
Butter (for cooking and baking)
Almond milk (if required)

Nuts & Seeds

Chia seeds (for pudding)
Walnuts or almonds (for salads or toppings)

Fruits

Bananas (for toffee)
Berries (blueberries for trifle, others if needed)
Apples (for baking)
Lime (for avgolemono soup and garnish)

Pantry Staples

Olive oil
Coconut flour (if needed for pancakes)
Baking powder (if required)
Vanilla extract
Spices (paprika, black pepper, sea salt, saffron for paella)
Soy sauce (low sodium)
Balsamic vinegar (for dressing)
Stevia (for sweetening desserts)
Canned white beans (for tuna salad)
Canned tomatoes (if required)

Rice (for paella)
Coconut milk (for fish stew)

Miscellaneous

Unsweetened dark chocolate (if needed for desserts)
Gelatin (if needed for desserts)
Mustard (for beef medallions)
Cocoa powder (if needed for desserts)
Lemon juice (for various dishes)
Chickpea or buckwheat flour (if required for pancakes)
Pomegranate juice (if needed for dressing)

Grocery Shopping List for 8-14 Day Meal Plan

Proteins

Oats (for baked oatmeal)
Pork (for herb-crusted pork and other pork dishes)
Red fish (for patties)
Couscous
Eggs (for omelet)
White fish (for creamy garlic sauce dish)
Beef (for braised beef and minestrone)
Turkey (for stuffed bell peppers)
Shrimp (for Cajun dish)
Squid (for salad)
Ricotta cheese
Cottage cheese (for roll and toast)
Feta cheese (for omelet)
Mozzarella cheese (for salad)

Vegetables & Herbs

Zucchini (for baking and roasting)
Spinach
Mushrooms (for soup and salad)
Tomatoes (fresh and canned)
Bell peppers (for stuffing)
Cauliflower (for grits)
Fresh herbs (thyme, basil, parsley, etc.)
Garlic
Onions
Almonds (for quinoa dish and cookies)
Walnuts (for oatmeal)
Capers (for chicken piccata)
Quinoa

Dairy and Dairy Alternatives

Milk (for oatmeal and other recipes)
Butter (for cooking and baking)
Heavy cream (for fish sauce)

Fruits

Apples (for baked oatmeal)
Berries (for oatmeal and sorbet)
Bananas (for candies)
Pears (for baking)
Lemons (for chicken piccata and other dishes)
Blueberries (for clafoutis)

Pantry Staples

Oatmeal
Dark chocolate (for truffles)
Almond flour (for cookies)
Cinnamon
Cocoa powder
Peanut butter (for baskets)

Baking ingredients (baking powder, sugar-free vanilla extract, etc.)
Spices (Cajun seasoning, black pepper, sea salt, etc.)
Olive oil
Soy sauce (if needed)
Whole grain or buckwheat flour (if required for muffins)

Miscellaneous

Honey or sweetener alternatives (sugar-free)
Lavash bread (for roll)
Tomato sauce or paste (for toast and other dishes)

Grocery Shopping List for 15-21 Day Meal Plan

Proteins:

Chicken (breast and drumsticks)
Lamb (for meatballs and skewers)
Duck breast
Fish fillets (for various recipes)
Shrimp
Squid
Mussels
Eggs
Ricotta cheese
Greek yogurt

Vegetables & Herbs:

Spinach
Tomatoes (cherry and regular)
Arugula
Zucchini
Red and green bell peppers
Onions (red and regular)

Garlic
Lemon and lime
Fresh herbs (thyme, parsley, dill, etc.)
Asparagus
Broccoli
Cucumbers

Fruits:

Berries (strawberries, blueberries, raspberries)
Bananas
Oranges
Dates
Pumpkin (for cheesecake)

Dairy and Dairy Alternatives:

Butter
Heavy cream
Mozzarella cheese
Parmesan cheese

Nuts & Seeds:

Assorted nuts (for smoothie and pancake filling)
Chia seeds
Peanut butter

Grains and Flour:

Buckwheat (for patties)
Quinoa
Oatmeal
Almond flour
Coconut flour

Pantry Staples:

Olive oil
Spices (cumin, paprika, cinnamon, nutmeg)
Sweeteners (for diabetic-friendly desserts)
Balsamic vinegar
Soy sauce

Honey (for keto sauce)
Canned pumpkin (for cheesecake)
Coconut milk

Miscellaneous:

Tzatziki sauce ingredients (cucumber, dill, garlic)
Dark chocolate (for truffles)
Gelatin (for cheesecake)
Capers (for chicken piccata)
Chimichurri sauce ingredients

Grocery Shopping List for 22-28 Day Meal Plan

Proteins:

Chicken (whole for stuffing)
Tuna steaks
Mussels
Shrimp
Ground beef (for Asian beef salad)
Pork (for soup and main dishes)
Eggs
Cottage cheese

Vegetables & Herbs:

Mushrooms
Spinach
Cauliflower
Avocado
Tomatoes (cherry and regular)
Kale
White beans
Bell peppers
Zucchini
Green onions
Garlic

Fresh herbs (thyme, parsley, cilantro, dill)

Fruits:

Blueberries
Apples
Lemons
Raspberries

Dairy and Dairy Alternatives:

Cheddar cheese
Mozzarella cheese
Heavy cream
Greek yogurt

Nuts & Seeds:

Walnuts
Chia seeds
Almonds (for granola)

Grains and Flour:

Buckwheat
Oatmeal
Coconut flour
Glass noodles (for stir-fry)

Pantry Staples:

Olive oil
Sesame oil (for Asian salad)
Spices (cumin, paprika, cinnamon, chili powder for Cajun seasoning)
Sweeteners (for diabetic-friendly desserts)
Balsamic vinegar
Soy sauce
Honey
Sesame seeds

Miscellaneous:

Coffee (for cheesecake)

Dark chocolate (for
cheesecake)
Gelatin (for cheesecake)

Tapenade ingredients (olives,
capers)
Paella rice

Made in the USA
Columbia, SC
22 October 2024

44886669R00041